Praise

If you've ever wondered how to make money in multifamily real estate, *Multifamily Apartment Syndications* has the answer. Written by veteran real estate investor Chris Roberts, the book provides a gripping account of both how to set up and run a real estate business and how Roberts and his partners made a tidy profit buying a rundown apartment building, fixing it up, and selling it for a handsome profit.

Dan Handford | Managing Partner,
PassiveInvesting.com

A surprisingly engrossing read. For those who think learning how to buy, rehab, and sell multifamily real estate at a profit can't be entertaining—as well as educational—sector expert Chris Roberts is here to prove them wrong. He skillfully weaves the story of how his company refurbished a decrepit Class C apartment complex and made it a safe, crime free place to live into the larger narrative of how investors can successfully invest in this asset class.

Rob Pene | Financial Freedom with Real Estate
Podcast Producer

If your goal is to make money in multifamily real estate property, I have 4 words of advice for you. Get this book now! Chris Roberts has successfully made money in flipping single family homes, purchasing, refurbishing and selling Class C "fixer upper" apartment buildings and investing in new construction luxury apartment buildings. *Multifamily Apartment Syndications*, his primary focus is on explaining how investors can form their own real estate company, build their credibility and buy, rehab, and sell multifamily properties or invest with experts in the field. Overall, an A+ effort from one of the country's foremost experts on multifamily real estate.

Michael Blank | CEO, Nighthawk Equity

I never knew how profitable multifamily real estate could be—or how much hard work it can take to make money in the field until I got started. — I read Multifamily Apartment Syndications and Chris is spot on.

Chris Roberts is a veteran real estate syndicator with numerous deals under his belt, and he doesn't sugarcoat the hard work that goes into fixing up a dilapidated apartment building to make it a decent place to live. Besides making tenants feel safe, bettering the community in this way creates value for investors, which can enable them to, ultimately, sell out at a profit. He provides an absorbing account of the details involved: attracting investors, negotiating a deal, hiring contractors, dealing with tenants, and putting the property on the market.

All in all, this book is a fascinating primer for anyone contemplating investing in the multifamily real estate sector or interested in learning the ins and outs of the business."

Drew Kniffin | President, Nighthawk Equity

This is a phenomenal book! Chris Roberts spares no detail in explaining how to buy, fix up and sell multifamily real estate for fun (that is, if you consider hard work fun!) and profit. Having done just this many times, he provides an expert's insight into each step of the process, from scouting out properties to negotiating to buy them, working with contractors to fix them up and then putting them on the market when the time is right. Highly recommended for would-be multifamily real estate investors.

Ruben Greth | BTR Subdivision Developer, Managing Partner at Legacy Acquisitions, Host of The Capital Raiser Show

If you're looking to get started in multifamily syndications, look no further. Chris Roberts is a leading authority in buying, rehabbing, and selling apartment buildings, and in *Multifamily Apartment Syndications*, he reveals his battle-tested secrets and creative insider strategies for transforming a multifamily property into a profitable asset.

Annie Dickerson | Founder & Chief Brand Officer, Goodegg Investments

If you're looking for a get rich quick scheme, look elsewhere, but if you're willing to put in a lot of hard work—or invest with someone who does—multifamily real estate can be a great place to invest. That is the message delivered by real estate investor extraordinaire Chris Roberts. In *Multifamily Apartment Syndications*, he details how you can make money by buying troubled multifamily complexes, then rehabbing them and selling them when the time is right.

Doug Walker | Real Estate Broker, John L. Scott, Inc.

I have tremendous admiration for Chris, both as a business operator and as an individual. He has found his true calling, utilizing his exceptional talents to empower others in their pursuit of retirement goals.

This concise book serves as an extension of Chris's impactful work. It effortlessly captures his experiences in a nonintimidating manner, presenting readers with invaluable insights and golden nuggets on real estate Investments.

Michael Lin | Managing Partner, HoneyPot Investments

Chris has created an honest look into what it takes to succeed in real estate syndication. By reading this book you'll learn what it takes to succeed in the ever-changing world of real estate, where deals can take drastic turns overnight. Chris and Sterling Rhino Capital are providing an honest view of the nitty-gritty of getting big deals across the finish line and delivering strong returns for your investors.

Taylor Loht | Founder, NT Capital

ACQUISITION FLOW CHART

Please click below to receive your free copy
of the Acquisition Flow Chart
promised with the purchase of the book.

Download FREE Flow Chart HERE

Thank you for ordering.
We hope this chart will be helpful to you.

CHRIS ROBERTS

Multifamily Apartment Syndications

The Truth About Buying and Selling Your First Value-Add Building

By Chris Roberts

Leaders
Press

Leaders
Press

ISBN **978-1-63735-236-6** (paperback)
ISBN **978-1-63735-235-9** (ebook)

Library of Congress Control Number: **2023907782**

Table of Contents

Table of Contents

Preface

I've often asked people, "What does retirement for you look like?" It can be a surprising question because I think people generally focus solely on, "I want to retire. I can't wait to leave my job," or whatever it may be. I'll ask them, "What do you really want to do in retirement?"

Here are a few things people say: "I want to spend time with my family," "I want to watch my kids grow up," "I want to spend time with my parents," or "I want to spend time enjoying the things I love, like going on vacations or doing my crafts." I've even heard this: "I'm not sure exactly what I want to do. I just want to be free." One thing I hear people say a lot is, "I just want to be free to choose." I love that. When I talk about a purpose-driven life, I ask people, "What does that mean to you? What does it mean to live a purpose-driven life?" Because if you can identify what it means to live a purpose-driven life, then you can use that to focus and drive you to start a business, build stronger relationships, or spend your nonproductive time learning, and this will help you achieve your goals a lot quicker. This will help you identify what you might do in retirement or why you're pushing to get there.

You have to find and focus on something that inspires you every day, and the only way you're going to have that is if you are identifying what it is exactly you want to do when you retire. What's interesting is, a lot of people don't want to retire and do nothing—they just want to have the freedom to choose the things they want to do. I encourage people to think about how much freedom they will have to go out and create and live their best second life, their best purpose-driven life after that initial retirement. So I find learning about that aspect of the retirement equation interesting when we talk to people about it.

I find that if you can use an emotional attachment and plant it in your own mind, if you can attach the emotion of having that purpose-driven life, living a life of freedom, doing the things you love, spending more time with your family (because we're only on this earth for so long), then that can drive you to do the right things with your finances early on. It can enable you to create those multiple streams of income that pay you while you sit on a beach, do your crafts, volunteer in your community, or while you watch your kids grow—it'd be completely your choice!

So what does it take to create financial freedom in multifamily real estate?

Shots fired, drug deals gone wrong, an unpermitted reno-vation, tons of deferred maintenance, and a horde of angry tenants.

It's perfect! Where do I sign? Let's get started!

Don't worry. You will likely not face all of these obstacles when starting a *real estate syndication* business, but I will share a story of a project where we did face all these challenges.

Now I know what you're thinking. Why would anyone actually look at a multifamily deal in a neighborhood riddled with crime, shady dealings, and a whole host of issues? If not, you should be.

Well, it's simple. As an investor, you don't know what you don't know, and if you don't push yourself beyond what you thought you were capable of, as our friend Jack Canfield says, "You will never get to the other side of fear." You must follow the data and negotiate the best deal so you can overcome most of the obstacles you may be presented with. Don't let emotion or fear drive your decisions. The good news is someone has done it before you. They have dealt with the same challenges you will face, so you need to learn from their experiences.

That's not to say this type of property is the only way to go. I have diversified my investments into many types of properties, including luxury new development, but these challenged properties should not be overlooked. They can provide a great opportunity to build a better neighborhood for the community and turn around the lives of the children who live there. There are great profits to be made for sure, but you do so much more for the community, tenants, and investors when turning properties like these around. Relax, it's not as bad as it sounds.

Multifamily real estate investment opportunities can create passive income and build equity. When done right, it is considered one of the best types of high-return investments.

Cash flow, wealth, and—eventually—freedom are not usually just handed to us. They must be earned. Every challenge is just an opportunity waiting to present itself. Success is earned through hard work, determination, and perseverance. Outwork your competition, and it's likely you will eventually succeed.

Getting started and taking action every day is the most important part, but doing it with a challenged property in your sights can teach you a lot early on, and it may put you in a position to deal with almost anything that comes your way.

Now, obviously, every property is not worth your time and energy. But in some cases, beneath a rough exterior is a diamond. You just have to be willing to find it.

Consider this statement when fighting your mind to move forward through your challenges:

"I am not a victim of my environment or my circumstances, but I am the results of my actions and my attitude. I don't have time for fear in my life because I'm achieving my dreams."

Having the correct mindset, vision, or mantra can make all the difference in the world in keeping you focused on what's important.

—Chris Roberts, founder and CEO,
Sterling Rhino Capital

Introduction

In this book, my objective is to provide a broad account of how you can make money as an investor/operator in multifamily real estate. The focus is on the opportunities offered by apartment buildings, mainly value-add deals (properties that need some work or have upside to renovate so you can increase the income, which, in turn, increases the value, hence value-add), but with a bit about investing in new construction as well. I write from extensive experience in this sector, not only as a hands-on operator and investor of my own capital, but also as a passive investor. The largest part of the book will consist of a detailed description—from start to finish—of one of the many value-add deals that my team and I have bought, renovated, and sold as multifamily investors and entrepreneurs.

A multifamily property is any type of building or group of buildings that can accommodate more than one family. A multifamily property can be a duplex, a two-family building, all the way up to a five-hundred-unit apartment complex that can house hundreds of families. Any building or complex with five or more units is termed a "commercial" multifamily.

At Sterling Rhino Capital, we seek out and buy large commercial multifamily, value-add apartment buildings, and we also build them from the ground up. We do this with equity raised through our passive investors with a mission to provide higher-than-average returns for those investors when compared to the S&P 500. These returns come in the form of cash flow dividend payments while we own and operate the complex, combined with profits from the sale of the property. In most cases, investors can also participate in utilizing the depreciation in the buildings, offering some potential tax advantages as well.

We could not succeed in these efforts without many considerations, such as protecting our investors with conservative underwriting and preserving their capital while maximizing their returns, how to negotiate the best possible recession-resistant deal, how to navigate the worst-case scenarios that can (and do!) occur, and how to stress-test the deal to cope with potential changes in the economy and environment.

I will start by outlining some considerations when thinking about retirement or leaving a W2 job to pursue a real estate profession. Many use these as motivation when starting a syndication business or even considering passive investing in real estate. I will cover some basics of investing in general, review what motivated me when I decided to exit my profession to pursue a real estate career and talk a bit about "Unlikely Mentors." We'll discuss a number of steps that budding real estate sponsors or syndicators can take to prepare themselves for turning around value-add apartment buildings. I'll also cover some important aspects of getting started, such as creating your company and establishing your brand. After that, the book will take an in-depth look at the ground floor details of what it takes to make money in value-add multifamily real estate using a real case study of a deal my team and I negotiated, closed, and eventually sold while exceeding our projected returns. My goal is to highlight a few of the key elements you should have in place from the start when developing your business model and how to navigate through some of the issues that may come up during the negotiation and due diligence period. This will help you better prepare to move through your deal from a position of strength to a solid close.

After the deal closes, the work of turning around an under-performing complex begins. The book covers in detail how to handle everything from unexpected setbacks to dealing with troublesome tenants and flaky contractors. It also explains how improving the property for the tenants paves the way for adding value, both for them and the operators and their investors. Finally, we arrive at the sale of the property, when the value added by the turnaround is booked in the form of significant profits. After discussing takeaways from the value-add deal that is the book's primary focus, in the final chapters we take a high-level look at investing in and developing apartment buildings from the ground up, starting a fund, and what my company is doing in this space.

What You Will Learn

Some of what we will discuss includes the following:

- Why you should focus on raising money early.
- Making sure your company has a solid brand, a good thought-leadership platform, and a social-proof presence.
- The pros and cons of investing in neighborhoods with higher-than-average crime and what you can do to enhance the tenants' safety and experience while living there.
- How to identify the right person on your team to negotiate and communicate with brokers or sellers on the deal.
- Always assume the seller is hiding something. What is it?

- Never assume things are set in stone or that you can't ask for more.
- Be fair, but know your numbers. Look at how you can leverage your knowledge during due diligence.
- Execute your plan like a leader and assume no one understands your angle. Sell your position to everyone and stay on top of everything.
- How to deal with unforeseen issues *after* closing your deal.
- How you can outperform your pro forma.
- How to sell your property once you have delivered on your promise to your investors.
- Why it can make sense to diversify into new construction multifamily, and some considerations for investing in this asset class.
- Starting a fund to raise capital.

Chapter 1
The Basics of Investing

When you start working, you're probably told by someone that it's important to save. Usually, we're told to save by at least putting a little money away. When you do that, you could put some money in a savings account or leave it in your checking account, but typically, you're only going to get somewhere between .25% to maybe 1% return on that money. It might be a bit higher now that rates have been rising, but not all that much. While it's liquid (you can pull it out at any time, you can spend it, and you have access to it), that's not a very good return.

One place to put your money is in a simple tax-advantaged account like an IRA (individual retirement account). This is an account set up to invest your funds in mutual funds, stocks, or CDs, some of which are traded in the stock market. This is typically where you put money that is for long-term investing. You don't typically pull these funds out as they can be subject to tax and penalties if withdrawn early. This forces you to be patient and not withdraw funds or profits until you are in your sixties. Oftentimes, you can invest two different ways into a retirement account. You can contribute to a Roth IRA, which basically enables you to contribute money you've earned after you have paid taxes on it but gain tax advantages down the road.

In other words, you don't have to pay any taxes on those gains when you withdraw money from your Roth IRA. Or you can contribute that money in what they call a traditional IRA. You could see some tax deductions for the funds you contribute for the tax year in which they are contributed, and any gains are tax-deferred, but you will be taxed on any funds you withdraw down the road.

Now there's nothing wrong with those types of retirement plans. As a matter of fact, in a tax-advantaged account such as a 401(k), sometimes you can get your employer to contribute anywhere from .25% to 5% of the amount you invest. So there's some incentive there. But the problem with this type of vehicle for building a nest egg is that, using roughly over a hundred years of past performance, on average, you might see from 7% to 8% returns in that type of investment. Then you have fees that are taken out of that. Now this is assuming your 401k is investing that money into the S&P 500 or some other stock index. So your net returns might be lower than 5% to 6% when it's all said and done. Not only that, but with a few exceptions, you can't touch that money whatsoever until you're at least fifty-nine and a half—well, at least without severe penalties from Uncle Sam. Often, people don't withdraw from their IRAs until they're much older than that. So it's a fairly illiquid asset. It's sitting there, in most cases, in the stock market, which is where a lot of retirement accounts get invested. You can't take it out, because if you do, you'll be taxed and maybe even penalized on top of that.

Here are some interesting investing statistics from Financiallysimple.com.[1]

1. If you do not start saving until forty-five, you will need to save three times as much as if you start at twenty-five.
2. About 90% of actively managed funds underperformed passive funds.

3. About 0.75% in fees equates to a 20% smaller nest egg in just thirty years.

4. On average, women invest more conservatively than men.[2] Over the long run, this can result in lower returns and more of a risk of your assets not keeping pace with inflation.

5. A long-term asset return study by Deutsche Bank stated the last time interest rates were near current levels (the 1950s), Treasury Bonds lost 40% of their inflation-adjusted value over the following three decades.[3]

6. In August 2000, *Fortune* magazine published "10 Stocks to Last the Decade."[4] By December 2012, a portfolio containing those 10 stocks lost 74.3% of its value.

7. All economists agree that predicting a stock's price is tough. However, only 59% of Americans agree with that statement.

8. On average, women earn 82% of what men bring home.[5]

9. Around 40% of stocks fell at least 70% since 1980.[6] That's considered "catastrophic losses," and they never recovered.

10. *Vanguard* reported that of all the mutual funds benchmarked to the S&P 500, 72% underperformed the index over a twenty-year period, which ended in 2010. The phrase "professional investor" is certainly a loose one when looked at through the lens of the history of stocks.

11. Most people expect to have their mortgage paid off by the age of seventy-five However, 21% of Americans still carry a mortgage debt at that age.

12. The average retirement account generates less than $400 per month for income in the "Golden Years."

Perception is not reality when you're playing with money. Get to the facts, and base your investing decisions on careful planning and solid data.

Some common investment vehicles are low-yield or high-yield savings accounts, money market accounts, the stock market (includes all equities, ETFs, mutual funds), commodities, digital currencies, and real estate. All of these things can be invested inside a retirement account or outside a retirement account. Now, full disclosure, I am not a financial advisor or a CPA. I am giving you some things to consider and encourage you to learn more and to seek out professionals for advice so they can assess your specific situation and advise accordingly. Do your research before investing your hard-earned money into these, and map out a plan as to how you will reach your retirement number.

For a bit more on retirement planning, consider this excerpt from an article, titled "Workers Are Dangerously Under-estimating How Much Income They Need to Replace in Retirement" from Fool.com.[8]

> Don't leave yourself with too little money to live on!
>
> When you retire and are no longer getting a paycheck, you need to replace the income your employer used to provide you. As you set retirement goals, determining how much of your income you need to replace is key—specially as most people's spending changes in retirement.[9]
>
> Unfortunately, many people aren't being realistic when they're estimating the amount of their pre-retirement income they'll need to cover their costs in their later years. And that can be a huge problem because if

you set your sights too low and plan to live on an unrealistic budget, you could find yourself struggling as a retiree or drawing down your investment accounts too quickly.

They go on to say that most people surveyed thought they only needed about 66% of their current income while in retirement. But experts say that you actually need closer to 80%. This is according to recent research presented by the Transamerica Center for Retirement Studies in an article.[10]

Investing in Real Estate

What's great about real estate is there are different ways you can invest in it. It's very flexible; you can be an active investor, or you can be a passive investor. So let's talk a bit about passive investing.

A passive investor is anyone who owns shares but does not participate in the day-to-day decisions of running the company. Passive investing is not limited to real estate. Investing in the stock market is considered a passive investment. If you were to passively invest in real estate, you would take a specific amount, anywhere from, let's say, a thousand dollars in a crowdfunding platform, all the way up to hundreds of thousands, if not millions, of dollars you want to invest. Now you can invest directly into new development, multifamily apartments, storage units, mobile home parks—there are all kinds of assets you can invest in—and even triple net retail, carwashes, you name it. You have many options. You're a non-active investor, a passive investor. So you take some money, you put it in with a group of people, and you'll get a projected cash flow return for that investment, let's say, somewhere around 7%. But this is only part of your return on that investment.

You really have three advantages to investing passively in these types of assets. For the most part, you'll get cash flow first, which is nice. It's kind of equal to what you would get in the form of dividends if you invested in a 401K or IRA. Sometimes, those will invest your money into the stock market. Some of the companies it invests in may pay out what they call a dividend, and typically, it could be anywhere from 1% to 5%. It's basically like a share of profits, if you will. But again, you are not only taxed on these dividends; you also can't spend that money without being penalized by the IRS (Internal Revenue Service) if your traditional retirement account is investing in the stock market.

Now in multifamily apartments, storage units, or many of these other tangible types of investments, you can get this distribution payment, which is a share of profits or a share of the income the asset is producing. Not only that, but you also get a portion of any appreciation of the asset you own a piece of. So if they create the appreciation through a value-add play, let's say, renovating, fixing things up—again, this could be on any of these asset classes—you also get a piece of that when they sell the assets, a piece of the appreciation based on the value of the asset when they sell. That could be worth anywhere from, let's just say, for argument's sake, 6% to 12% or even more above and beyond the cash flow distributions you received. So you could see a combined return somewhere between, let's say, 15% and 20%, sometimes higher, versus what I was saying earlier, where you might see 6% to 8% overall return in the S&P 500 after fees.

I recently read an article in *U.S. News & World Report* that detailed some of the advantages to investing in multifamily real estate versus single-family houses or the stock market.[11] Below is an insert from that article:

How to Invest in Multifamily Real Estate

Apartment rentals can trump single-family rentals for investors.

Investing in multifamily properties, like apartment complexes, can offer a path to passive wealth generation that bypasses the volatility of stock market movements.[12]

"Multifamily has been one of the most attractive and desirable investment property types for investors during the current cycle," says Russ Moroz, first vice president of investments at Marcus & Millichap.

It's popularity, Moroz says, can be attributed largely to perceived stability in the housing market and consistent growth in both demand and rental rates for multi-unit properties.

Multifamily investing yields several clear-cut benefits, beyond those associated with single-family home rentals.

Raphael Sidelsky, chief investment officer at W5 Group in New York, says those benefits include a solid risk-return profile, cash flow, and capital appreciation. Multifamily housing also benefits from declining rates of homeownership, a trend Sidelsky says is likely to persist for the foreseeable future. [14]

The article goes on to explain how crowdfunding sites can give easy access to investors with lower barriers to entry when seeking out a real estate investment. You can learn more about crowd funding at Silicon Prairie.

Now that you're in the know about what you can invest in, next up for review is another advantage to investing in real estate: depreciation.

What Is Depreciation, and Why Is It Important to an Investor?

Depreciation has two main aspects. The first aspect is the decrease in the value of an asset over time. The second is allocating the price you originally paid for an expensive asset over the period of time you use that asset. Now the investors get a share of depreciation as LPs (limited partners). So as an LP, you get a share of the depreciation when the government allows you to take a tax deduction against the asset. You should always discuss this with your CPA because how much you can take advantage of this is based on your specific circumstances, but real estate is a great tax shelter in general. That's because you renovate these properties, and you invest money into them. Thus, you get the opportunity to take depreciation or offset your taxes or your passive income with that depreciation. So you get three benefits: you get distributions, or what some call cash flow; you get a share of any upside equity; and you get depreciation, which could lower your taxes. So if those distributions are coming back to you and you invested cash, you can spend that money, which is great. These are projections, not guarantees, and proper due diligence should always be applied when considering any kind of investing.

An active investor, on the other hand, is anyone who actively participates in the day-to-day activities of running the company. An example of this in real estate would be a landlord.

You're considered an active investor, which means you have to deal with the toilets, tenants, termites, and all that comes with owning a building occupied by humans. Not a lot of people want that. Or if you're an active investor in multifamily, mobile home parks, or commercial retail, you are part of a general partnership team that now manages that asset. Again, dealing with tenants, toilets, property managers, renovations, and construction—all that stuff makes you an active investor.

As a general partner of a syndication team, you have a tremendous amount of responsibility, You're also held accountable by lender-required "Bad Boy" clauses in your Private Placement documents. You can't just go and run off with your investors' money, or you can get into big, big trouble—Federal Prison trouble. You have a tremendous amount of responsibility and are accountable to your investors and partners and must execute at a high level—this is a lot of work.

Now the benefit of being a general partner is you are compensated by managing that asset for all of the investors/limited partners. There's a lot of work involved, but you and the team are compensated by getting a share of ownership of the deal and a share of some of the distribution payments and/or asset management fees. You could also use the asset management fees to hire an asset manager.

So that's a basic account of how investments work with stocks, multifamily, and other types of assets as an investor, limited partner, and general partner.

Chapter 2
My Great Escape

My career in the real estate business was a process—it didn't happen all at once. No one teaches us about real estate in school, and it's not talked about after you graduate either. So how do you learn?

We were told the American dream was to buy a house, but we were not taught how to invest. Okay, so you go buy a house. Unfortunately, I bought my house in 2006, a few years before the stock market crashed, and its value was around $280,000. Then a year or so later, the real estate market crashed in 2007, and I thought I had way overpaid for the house. I watched my value dive down by about $80,000 to around $200,000 and thought, *Oh my gosh, the American Dream, it's crushed*. But I was patient, and I hung in there. And it's interesting—that same home is now worth about $550,000, which is way more than I paid for it. So it came back. While a lot of people got foreclosed on, gave up, and ran, I just hung in there. I'm, like, "Well, hopefully, it comes back." And it did, which is, I think, revealing. You cannot get caught up in that panic mode. If anything, learn more about the historical trends and how recessions and interest rate swings really affect the economy and real estate long term.

I went back to analyze that first single-family residence that I still own today and compared it to a sixteen-year average in my retirement portfolio that consisted of target retirement funds and stocks, and it was crystal clear. My single family home crushed the returns in my retirement portfolio. The short version is this: If I were to sell the home after sixteen years of owning it, I would have $330,000 in equity after tax. This includes some rental income, and after only putting down about $30,000 to purchase it. This is over a 22% return annually when compared to my retirement portfolio of 7.5% to 8%, and this was before management fees and after contributing over $125,000 into it. This is crazy—$30,000 for $330,000 in real estate versus $120,000 for $250,000 in my traditional retirement account!

So I knew there was some power in real estate. I just didn't know to what end, because I had invested in the stock market. So as I started making money, I invested a little bit of it in the stock market. I'd been doing that for about ten years, but it wasn't growing that substantially. I didn't know what a portfolio should look like. I didn't know how much money I should have. Nobody ever told me, "You need to put this amount of money aside, because you're going to need this amount of money when you get older. And it's going to grow at this rate of return." Again, even as an adult making great money, no one in my circle of influence cared to share advice on the value of investing. So here I am, mulling things over year after year after year, investing in my retirement plan, and talking to friends. Some people had $200,000, and some people had a million in their retirement plans or whatever, but no one ever talked about how that was relevant to how much they would need when they actually retired. They just said, "I have this amount of money." So I bought a few pieces of land as well. I sold them. I made a little bit of money just on a whim and still didn't understand the power of real estate.

Turning on the Light

So how did I find real estate to be my great escape? The first step was to realize that what I was currently investing in was unlikely to take me where I wanted to go from a financial and lifestyle perspective. I was what they call a "traditional investor." I was saving a little bit of money, and I was contributing to my retirement account. Then one day, I had a meeting with a friend of mine. He began talking to me about this rental income, and that's when the light bulb went on. It opened up my eyes to an investment vehicle that I had never really thought much about, even though I owned a single family residence. I had bought a little bit of land and sold it, but I was never in the rental real estate space. I thought that was too time-consuming. *There's no way I could do that*, I thought, and I just brushed it off. But he started to show me the amount of cash flow you can make that you can actually spend, and he talked a little bit about this depreciation thing. He went on to explain that you can build equity in these kinds of assets that grow while someone else pays down the debt. We mapped out the power of that equity over time, and there was no turning back. I had an incredible revelation. I could not believe I had been missing out for so long and all because I had not taken the time to explore, be curious, and allocate time outside my comfort zone.

So I got home, and I read all these real estate books, and it really started to make sense to me. I thought, *Man, after fifteen years of contributing to my retirement account, I only have so much money*. This seemed crazy to me. As I looked at this real estate model, I realized that with the appreciation, depreciation and cash flow, there was huge upside in this space. I realized that I needed to buy single-family rentals and start creating more streams of income through the cash flow from those rentals So I came home from that meeting and immediately read a bunch of real estate books. I started digging in and educating myself. I quickly realized that this was a model I could buy into.

This, of course, was after I had a meeting with my financial advisor, and the financial advisor knew nothing about real estate and kept pushing me toward the stock market and traditional IRAs. But the numbers the financial advisor was giving me didn't even come close to the numbers my friends who had these rental properties were getting. I realized I had to learn more about this. I dug in, I got on podcasts, I got on webinars, and I started learning. Then before it was popular to go and buy these programs to teach you how to do it, I started building my own spreadsheets to analyze market data.

In my experience, the people most likely to change your life are outside your existing circle of influence. They're not necessarily your friends, family, or immediate colleagues. What you need are what I call "unlikely mentors." Some of these unlikely mentors are the people who will help you to discover a piece of yourself you never knew existed. I took a lot of advice from some unlikely mentors along the way that guided me through sharing their stories as I shared mine. I realized there were a few markets in my own state that I could buy into, so I stayed focused on those. I bought more than a dozen single-family homes over about nine years at a cost of $100,000 to $150,000 each. I renovated, rented, and sold them for a profit. There is more to this story, but we are talking about multifamily syndications in this book, not single-family homes. I just wanted to give you a little backstory to lay the foundation.

I'm often asked, "Where do you start? How do you buy your first investment property?" The answer is not necessarily simple, so I'd like to highlight some things to consider as you dive into your first investment in a value-add rental property or new development project.

The same "Where do you start?" question can be asked about a multifamily real estate syndication company. The term *syndication* means "gathering resources." A real estate syndication brings people and their funds together to invest in a real estate asset. Instead of buying a bunch of small properties individually, like single-family homes, the group buys larger assets together, like a large apartment building. It's very difficult to start with no money, no reserves, and working a full-time job, but it can be done if you plan properly and build a good team.

If this description of my introduction to the real estate business doesn't make it seem easy—that's good, because it's not. In my view, the most common type of misinformation about this industry is that you can just get into it and be successful. The reason I say that is, of course, anyone who's willing to put in the work, anyone who's willing to put in the time, anyone who's willing to raise some money—sure, you can have some level of success in this space. But the misconception is that this is just some "quick fix, get rich" scheme. "Oh, buy a multifamily property, get rich, and be financially free!" And that all sounds great. It's not that it's not true at some level—you can be successful at it—but this is a business. It requires a tremendous amount of dedication, education, and sacrifice, just like any other business. You may have to work within this business as though it's a full-time job before you can work outside the business.

In other words, before you get to that level where you have all this cash flow coming in and you don't have to work, you will literally be creating a business from the ground up.

So the misunderstanding is that you can just go out and be successful. Yes, anyone is capable, in theory. But will they actually put in the work to do it? Then there's a little sidebar to that. I'm told, oftentimes, if you just find a deal, you can make it in this business. That's not necessarily true, in my opinion. I believe you need to be good with people and/or be able to raise money and be good at communicating and delivering value to others. This will put you in a position to take advantage of an opportunity that can springboard this career for you. Those are the two crucial ingredients for success, but the number-one cause of failure is that people don't treat this like a business. They think, *I just need to go find a property, and I can make it*, and that's not true.

My "Aha" Moment

My "aha" moment—or when I decided to go large and scale into commercial real estate—occurred when I realized it was time to exit corporate America a little bit quicker than I had planned. The only way to do that was to grow the portfolio and grow it fast and replace the income I was generating from that profession. The other thing was, I was really enjoying the real estate business.

So the "aha" moment arrived when I was listening to some podcasts about real estate and came across a multifamily investor group that not only owned large commercial real estate apartments but also taught people how to get into this space and scale their businesses. I realized that not only was it possible but there were also actual people who can teach you how to do it. From there, I quickly adopted a lot of those practices. I reached out to that individual and jumped into one of his programs to learn what he was doing. Two and a half years later, I was not only in a position of financial freedom but substantial growth as well. I was not about to let another opportunity to learn and advance pass me by as I did in single-family investing.

Being a previous business owner and knowing how to build business plans using a pro forma and having the knowledge of the overall structure of building a business, I applied all of that background to help in my real estate journey. You have overhead and invoices to pay, and many people are counting on you. There are a lot of moving parts. It was an "aha" moment when I realized how complicated it is to buy a larger commercial multifamily asset, and I was grateful I had passively invested in a few syndications, spent time in groups, and hired a mentor. Now I had owned single-family properties before, and that is kind of like owning a sole proprietorship or a small business. In business, you generally have a few employees, you lease a building, you have some invoicing and billing, and you're kind of on your way—you just need consumers to come in and buy your goods. In single-family property investment, you go to a lender, you apply for a loan, and the property's value is based on what your neighbors typically sell for. It's fairly easy to buy a property through a bank, as long as you have enough credit and enough down payment.

Whereas with commercial, my eyes were opened to the substantial amount of support you need, including a team of attorneys to handle all the legal filings. When you're doing a syndication, your legal documents can sometimes be 120 pages or more. You have also got property managers and a whole team of people you've got to deal with; you have your partners that you put together that are going to handle specific roles and goals like asset management, investor relations, systems and infrastructure, contractors, developers, or acquiring an existing building, etc. Then there's a whole bunch of other supporting cast members, including all the contractors that you have to deal with when you're renovating. So that's the long story short, but what was most eye-opening?

For me, the biggest surprise was how dynamic it actually is to acquire these commercial multifamily assets, and then how much work is involved after the fact. It's not like you just buy it, put all these people in place, and now you're just running around financially free, living on a beach. These are full-blown businesses—every single one of them. I knew that, but I had no idea how deep the rabbit hole went and how much work was going to be involved in managing these efficiently.

I went from my comfort zone of running some smaller businesses efficiently to multifamily, where I realized it was literally like multiplying our business process ten times; it was like dealing with five times the number of people—many more attorneys, CPAs, property managers, etc. It got far more dynamic. So the major shift was that when you scale, you also scale in your overhead, processes, systems, and workload. I've always been kind of a seven-day-a-week guy on call whenever my clients need me. But I found that I literally went from working, let's say, fifty to sixty hours a week to working like one hundred hours a week, because it was like I had two full-time jobs, with just a little bit of time for sleep and food. That was the way it was for several years. So that's where everything dramatically shifted because that's what I felt it was going to take to get this business off the ground and preserve the investors' capital. And we were very successful at it, fortunately, mainly because we had the right supporting staff, and the previous business experience and track record I had helped as well.

While I've discussed my "aha" moment, or moments, in some detail, I think it's important to add that for me, they were ultimately prompted by the epiphany that to escape the corporate grind in the first place—I needed to build a place to go. The realization hit me one day that I could lose my opportunity just because a new VP was hired, or some new management structures were being implemented. I was an independent business owner but relied on an annual contract for the bulk of my business, and any given year, I wasn't quite sure if I was going to get my contract renewed. You just don't have the security of building your own thing when you work for someone else or rely on a large contract. You never know if you're going to get pushed out or moved aside, or if a company is going to get acquired by somebody, so you have to go find something else to do. I saw this happen repeatedly to others, and it was not going to happen to me.

So there was that sort of fear and uncertainty, and I think the cool thing about transitioning into real estate was it not only created a substantial amount of wealth, financial freedom, and passive cash flow but also provided a little bit of extra security as now you have this other form of income beyond my normal workload. As a result, if something happens in my current environment, I have a security blanket. I have another business that's running that can create what is basically another job that's paying me.

So that was the Great Escape—having the fear instilled in me that there's no guarantees in life, and you could lose your job or contract at any minute and have no control over it. You don't need to do what I did and run a full-blown real estate investment/equity firm, but having passive investments can mitigate the risk and take the control away from your employer, putting your destiny in your hands. I scaled enough to escape the corporate grind for good and real estate investing made that happen. I retired from corporate America in my forties to do what I love.

What I did at the end of the day is transition into a new way of working by realizing that I could go build my own thing. I could stand on my own two feet with my own company and create this great passive cash flow and not have to worry about somebody coming in and buying me out or easing me out of a job. It's my company, and I run the show. If you build a syndication business and/or invest passively in real estate, you too can run the show and create that freedom, but it will take overcoming fear, and it will take commitment and discipline.

The Value of Unlikely Mentors

As I've mentioned, I was helped along the way by mentors and unlikely mentors who helped show me the ropes. So what's an unlikely mentor? Unlikely mentors provide a completely new perspective on who you are and what's possible for you. They'll help you get out of your own way, discover pieces of yourself you never knew existed, focus your priorities, and free you up to take action toward the life you really want. They are informal, not usually paid, and are outside your immediate circle of influence. You will typically engage them as someone who inspires you. From there, you develop an organic relationship with them. You draw them in with your positive attitude and energy. To learn more about unlikely mentors, visit Unlikelymentor.com.

I believe mentorship, whether informal through sharing of stories or in the form of a program you purchase, is critical for you to have as a support system. You can find yourself and expose areas of opportunity you never knew were there. Oftentimes, you may not realize there are missing pieces in your process. For example, you may be a go-getter and ambitious, but you may not be very good at building out systems and structures or even a business. In my case, I had previous entrepreneurial experience. I was a business owner, and I had a lot of ambition and energy. But I needed to make sure that I was not going to make any mistakes that could cost me and my investors or partners a substantial amount of money. So hiring a mentor allowed us to scale more quickly and more efficiently.

I've had mentors who were paid and unlikely mentors who were organically introduced into my life on a personal and professional level, and I attribute some of the success I've had to their input. I've talked quite often about how having an unlikely mentor who taught me about finances, and reading books and educating myself and building a strong work ethic helped me learn how to be a successful entrepreneur. But on a specific topic, like multifamily real estate, it's also good to explore hiring a mentor, because they're going to help you on the specifics related to acquisition and execution. They won't just mentor you in general, but they can say, "Hey, here's how you use this model. Here's how you grow, and here are the puzzle pieces to put in play. And by the way, here's someone that's going to support you throughout the entire process."

In my opinion, mentors are vital to anyone's growth if they want to scale faster with more support. Check out what Patricia Duchene, a contributor at *Forbes*, wrote about the values mentors share:[14]

> In virtually any industry, having a mentor can be the catalyst for enriching career development. Mentors not only bestow real-life lessons and skills upon their mentees, but also open doors to professional networks, facilitating connections to other professionals who can help shape career success.

Here is the list of her five values great mentors share:

Accessibility

First and foremost, a good mentor is an available one. The last thing you'd want is to have your time and effort wasted if a mentor is unable to commit to engaging with you regularly. You need a mentor who is able to dedicate time to your development without being distracted by their own projects.

Authenticity

It's not enough to have accumulated degrees, titles, and years of experience to be a good mentor. They must be genuinely interested in helping you on your journey because they see your potential and want to help bring it to fruition. Truly great mentors don't want a carbon copy of themselves. Rather, they want to guide you in your discovery of what's possible based on your own talents and drive.

Objectivity

A good mentor is not going to spend time trying to be your best friend, nor should you seek that. Real growth in any profession means receiving honest feedback and learning from things that at first you may not want to hear, but will be essential to your long-term development.

Continual learning

Does your potential mentor seem stuck in their ways because "that's the way it's always been done?" Or are they open to new ideas and continually learning about their field? Ideally, your mentor is someone who has been in your field for a substantial amount of time, at least 10 to 12 years.

Values

Be aware that a highly successful person isn't always a person with strong core values. A mentor is someone you admire and respect, not only for their accomplishments but how they carry themselves and the way in which they treat others.

At the same time, mentors may not necessarily be for everybody. If you have a really strong personality and are not open to learning, they may not be a good fit. Some people don't want to scale faster, they want to take their time, they want to roll slow, or they're set in their ways. Maybe they don't need mentors. But we learn from those who have been there and done that. As a result, from my experience, I find that mentors can help us get there a lot faster, with more efficiency and all while mitigating risk. So if you are one of those strong personalities, I encourage you to flex a bit and be open to their skills and experience—doing so will benefit you in your endeavors.

Chapter 3
Raising Money

Why You Should Focus on This Early in the Process

I'm starting with raising money because this is one of the important—maybe even the most important—aspects of starting and running a multifamily real estate business. I have seen many people when they're starting out underestimate how challenging this can be, and some of them have paid big time for it.

Some things to consider when you begin to raise for your first deal: Set realistic money-raise expectations for yourself and/or your team. It's reasonable to set a goal of $250,000 per person on the team, so if you have four people, your group can raise $500,000. That's right; it's not $1 million. This is because you will likely only raise half of what you think. So instead of $1 million, it's $500,00 you will likely raise, especially on your first deal. If you only raise $500,000, then the target purchase price of your first deal should only be $1.2 to 1.5 million.

Remember, everyone on your team is always raising money. This raise on this deal will give you some room for closing costs, unforeseen changes by your lender, and some emergency reserves, but this is just an example. But take it seriously, as I have seen people commit to $250,000 and raise $0. I've also seen commitments of $250,000, and some of those people raised over $700,000. If you don't have a group of people in your circle that are capable of investing, then find someone on your team that can make up the difference or maybe someone that is in a professional network with coworkers or high-income earners that could invest. You could have a small group presentation for a few of them.

How to Begin Talking with Potential Investors

After you educate yourself about the process and begin to build a little confidence through the educational materials you gather early in the process, which we'll talk about in the next chapter, you can start having conversations with the people you know best, like friends and family. Once you get comfortable with explaining what a syndication is and how real estate investing works, you can branch out to others who are not in your immediate circle of influence. The more people you talk to, the more confident you will become. If you start by investing yourself in someone else's syndication, you can speak from experience. If not, then you could start by talking about the many benefits of investing in real estate that you've read about.

It's important to be conversational and not try to sound like you are selling them something. These investments are an opportunity to be part of something truly special and are not available to everyone, especially nonaccredited investors. If you build enough value in what you are offering, then some will invest with you. It's a good idea to record a few of your phone or Zoom calls so you can get feedback from others as you improve your process.

Don't be disappointed if you come in lower than your goal. You should use this as an opportunity to test your presentation and improve. Remember to share what you are doing with everyone you meet, and you will widen your span of influence as you grow.

If you can raise money, you can find real estate opportunities to buy or partner on, but finding deals does not mean you will find money to invest in them. I hear it time and time again that there is a ton of money out there looking for a home, but in my experience, it's expensive money and hard to lock in. Focus on your plan and work it, and you will be successful one opportunity and one investor at a time. Paul Esajian, a contributor at FortuneBuilders.com, detailed some sources to raise capital, as shown below: [15]

How To Raise Capital for Real Estate Investing: 8 Techniques

Real estate ventures need one thing, perhaps more than anything else: funding. Raising money for real estate deals is of the utmost importance, and it can be argued that it's the foundation of every deal. Therefore, investors must familiarize themselves with the most efficient ways to receive appropriate funding and gain access to it at a moment's notice. Note that learning how to raise capital for real estate is not as hard as it may seem — you need to know where to look.

The reality is venture capitalists are ready and willing to lend their money to those who can give them a solid return. Should you choose to pursue real estate investing, your mission is to convince these investors that you can provide a solid return. Venture capitalists will often gauge investment viability on one thing and one thing only: you. As the person asking them for money, you must be ready to convince them beyond a shadow of a doubt that you are worth their time and money.

While there are plenty of ways to secure working capital, there are six sources investors have come to rely on more than any others:

Private & Hard Money Lenders
Self-Directed Accounts
Private Placement Memorandums
Wholesaling
FHA Investment Loan
Peer-to-Peer Loan
Crowdfunding
Home Equity

Private and Hard Money Lenders

"Hard money" is a loan from an individual or small institution, typically requiring around 12% to 15% interest. You may also be asked to pay some additional points (interest that's paid upfront). That means interest on a hard-money loan is about three times higher than a traditional bank. The good news is hard money lenders require much less red tape than a bank and provide almost immediate access to capital. These lenders are actively looking for investments and usually make lending decisions based on the quality of the subject property, which may attract borrowers with less-than-perfect credit scores.

Self-Directed Accounts

Many folks with retirement accounts are not aware they can use those funds to make real estate investments without a penalty for early withdrawal. This applies to both individual retirement accounts (IRAs) and 401(k)s. These investment accounts must be held by a custodian, which helps set up and administer the self-directed account. Several rules guide the process, such as all profits must be returned to the self-directed account, but the profits will grow tax deferred.

Private Placement Memorandums

Similar to a private offering, a private placement memorandum (PPM) provides a means for an entrepreneur to describe the specifics of their opportunity to a number of potential investors. If successful, the PPM will entice investors, and the borrower will raise capital by selling securities to the investor.

Wholesaling

Wholesaling occurs when an investor sells a property, so it may seem odd to be on a list of ways to obtain funding to buy properties. But it can be used as a strategy to exit a property quickly to obtain funds for the next project. Entrepreneurs will need access to a dependable buyers list, along with the specifics of what those buyers are looking for. Once aware of what those buyers want, a savvy investor can be on the lookout and turn a property quickly with a nice profit.

FHA Investment Loan

The Federal Housing Administration (FHA) provides loans designed to help people with low and middle incomes buy homes. But they can be used to invest in real estate too. The catch is the property must be the borrower's primary address. With multifamily housing, an entrepreneur can live in one unit while renting out the others. FHA does have specific requirements for a borrower's credit score and down payment.

Peer-to-Peer Loan

The internet has allowed for a significant increase in this kind of investing, where one investor loans funds directly to another. Many online platforms have been developed exactly for this purpose. As you might expect, everything from interest rates to loan amounts and several other requirements will vary by investor or even by the online platform you use.

Crowdfunding

Another funding strategy that's benefited greatly from the internet, crowdfunding allows multiple investors to contribute to a single project. Investors may invest various amounts and will receive profits based on what the investment generates and the amount they've contributed. Various online platforms exist, such as Silicon Prairie, Fundrise, RealtyMogul, and Groundfloor. All platforms should be investigated to see which is right for your project, considering payback periods, loan amounts, even data security of the site.

Home Equity

A home equity line of credit (HELOC) allows you to make use of your home's equity to pay for repairs or renovations at the property or to make another investment. First, you must own the property, and you'll need to factor in payback amounts and other requirements to ensure the investment is worthwhile.

In my opinion, number 9 should be friends, family, and coworkers for your first raise. Especially when you start out, you should focus on your close group. This also gives you the opportunity to work through areas of improvement with your presentation while receiving constructive criticism.

Chapter 4
Getting Started as a Multifamily Real Estate Syndicator

Establish Your Brand and Market Presence

Negotiating a deal from a position of strength starts with your brand identity, reputation, and online market presence. Your brand identity basically answers the who, what, how, why, and where of your company. It establishes credibility by showing others that you know what you are doing and have the ability to close a deal.

A solid brand identity can help you stand out in a large crowd of other real estate companies and can help lay the foundation for establishing trust with sellers, brokers, and investors. Every new real estate investor lacks credibility when they are first starting out, which makes it harder to negotiate from a position of strength.

This is where your brand identity and online market presence comes in. Having a market presence (even the bare minimum!) is especially helpful in establishing your credibility. This could be as simple as having a good website and a social media platform and participating in podcast interviews while highlighting your business experience. You could also start your own podcast. We did this, and it made a huge difference in our business and assisted in educating our investors. Check out the CreateYourFortunePodcast.com, which is just one of our podcasts.

If you want some ideas on how you can start a podcast or expand your brand recognition, just follow the greats: Annie and Julie with Goodegg Investments, Michael Blank, Joe Fairless, Dan Hanford, Brad Sumrok, Neil Bawa, and Rod Khleif are some of the top multifamily thought leaders in the business today, and each has done an excellent job of building their brands through having an educational platform, market presence, and building solid teams around them. There are also many companies online that can produce your podcast for anywhere from $100 to $200 per episode. Many of the real estate educators above also offer mentor programs, and having personally been a member of a couple of them, I can tell you it was well worth it. You do not want to go at this without the proper education and support structure.

Building a strong market presence does not take a lot of time, but it does require consistency. Here are some nonnegotiables when establishing your market presence:

- I recommend you build a website, even if it's just a landing page. Start by setting up a domain name through a company like GoDaddy, and then you can build a basic website using a WordPress-based platform, but there are many hosting companies and site platforms to choose from. You should have a blog page that contains at least a few articles on multifamily investing and an "About Me" or "Meet the Team" page with you and/or your team's profiles and contact info. You can have this page listed at the bottom of your website's landing page, but the about page is good for search engine optimization (SEO). You should also have a few videos on YouTube that you post on your page.

- Next, you'll want to set up a ".com" email. Again, you can use GoDaddy. There are others for this, but having a .com email looks more professional.
- Third, get active on real estate social media pages on Facebook, LinkedIn, and Instagram. Join some of the local meetups and/or go to a few larger multifamily seminars, like Michael Blank's Deal Maker Live, Joe Fairless's Best Ever Conference, or the many others that exist in the multifamily apartment investing space. Here you can network and learn all there is to know about syndications from experts, not just in multifamily real estate, but also from many other types of real estate like storage units, build-to-rent single-family homes, mobile homes parks, new development, and more.

If all else fails, partner with someone who has an already established market presence, such as a family member, mentor, business counterpart, or a deal sponsor. The main point here is that a cohesive brand identity and market presence is nonnegotiable *before* you start negotiating multifamily deals, if you're going to have any meaningful success. When you start, it can be hard to land a deal, and having connections or partnering up can demonstrate you have it together. This also comes in handy when you are asked for proof of funds when one of your letters of intent is accepted. Many sellers will ask for that even though they know you are likely raising the money for the deal once you go under contract. It's a way of testing you, but the financials of a partner, a sponsor, or a key principal will work in place of liquid capital in your personal bank account.

At our business, what we set out to do is teach people how to retire early through real estate investing. We thought, okay, we found this great investing option, we've created wealth with single-family and multifamily in all these different vehicles in real estate. Now how do we share that with the world as we grow our business? Because if we focused *first* on how we help as many people as possible solve their problems and build real connections with them, investors and people would gravitate toward us because of our giving nature. And that just comes natural to us. We enjoy that. We get on a lot of podcasts and share a lot of information that we don't charge for. We participate in masterminds and Zoom meetups, and we often take phone calls from people who aspire to get into the space as sponsors. We found that this giving had a profound effect on our reputation early on.

Branding Experts

The branding experts I mentioned above can help you build your brand in a variety of ways. Julie and Annie with Goodegg Investments® are very good at teaching people how to build systems to develop their brands. As a matter of fact, we brought them on board to help us originally. They're very articulate and very good with video.

Michael Blank has a wonderful mentor program. He also offers various levels of training if you're not ready to hire a mentor. He is passionate about helping people become financially free. And he's unique in the way that he delivers that messaging.

Joe Fairless is a syndicator who also has some programs to further your education in multifamily real estate, but he also partnered with somebody who teaches about mindset.

What's great about this business is that it isn't just numbers. You must have the right mindset. You have to have the right level of confidence to grow. So Joe Fairless and his Best Ever brand have partnerships with people who are in his circle of influence. And they've grown substantially as a result of partnering.

Dan Hanford with the PassiveInvesting.com brand runs regular webinars to educate investors and leads a podcast interviewing syndicators that share their experience on their first real estate deals.

Brad Sumrok has a program where he actually assists his students in getting into the multifamily space through acquiring deals. He has a big training program as well that is somewhat unique. But I believe you have to buy into that deal flow within his exclusive network.

Neil Bawa is a numbers fanatic. He's a syndicator who, while he doesn't really have a mentor program, offers some educational info you can sign up for, and his analysis of markets and deals is second to none. You can learn a lot by following him because he's got a really, really good deal structure, and he uses the numbers and data to buy his assets.

Rod Khleif is a fired-up individual. He offers great two- or three-day training programs. He offers some mentor mastermind-type programs that are second to none. His energy level is unsurpassed. He talks a lot about how he lost millions of dollars during the crash and learned his lesson, then came back and grew substantially after that. He's just got a ton of energy and a humbling background; he also has a great podcast. So every one of these folks has a different way of teaching and growing. I think most people can learn a little bit of something from each of them. My team and I have as well as we've grown.

Getting Investor Testimonials

The results of building a strong brand and doing what you say you are going to do will build credibility. This can result in receiving great client testimonials. At my company, Sterling Rhino Capital, we started in the value-add space, and we built our credibility one deal at a time through hundreds and hundreds of investors and several key relationships, which allowed us to scale and expand into the new construction space. It's not easy to dive into the new construction space when you first start out—you must build your credibility in the business and partner with a top-notch developer. One thing you could work on early is building up your referrals. I recommend you get written and even video referrals if possible.

It's important that you communicate with your investors and ask them for referrals, because these are the type of folks that are going to come along with you when you get into, let's say, new construction, or maybe you're going from a class C to class A–type of property. They may not be used to it, but they're used to you. They're used to the way you treat them. They're used to the type of returns you give them, and most of all, you have developed a good communication system putting them at ease. If you do not have a top-notch way of communicating with your investors, you better get on it. This is extremely important.

In addition to referrals, testimonials can be a great way to show potential investors that you are not new to the business and demonstrate the success you have achieved. Having real people step up to say how happy they are with your services and your ability to make them money can be a powerful marketing tool.

For example, the following testimonials are from real investors who spoke about what we've been doing for them:

> "Chris and I have invested in five different deals with Sterling Rhino Capital. It has allowed us to let our money work for us while we sit on our beach in Mexico. For years, we have worked hard for our money—now our money is working hard for us. Thanks, Chris and Paul, you have helped us start our new chapter. Could not be happier." **(Pam E. and Chris K., Mexico)**

> "I strongly encourage anyone who is looking to build their wealth through passive real estate syndication, to let Chris and Paul and Sterling Rhino Capital guide them through the process. Whether it's your first time investing or not, Sterling Rhino makes the process extremely hassle-free and transparent. Our family understands the value of investing our extra funds in as many ways as possible in order to secure the best possible life for ourselves and our daughter later on in life. This was our family's first time making the decision to invest in passive real estate, so we were a bit nervous, but the entire process was so easy! And anytime we have a question, comment, or concern, Chris always responded with his time and knowledge to help us along the way. We plan on making more investments with Sterling Rhino Capital, along the rest of the way toward retirement. BIG thank you to Chris and Paul at Sterling Rhino Capital!" **(Devin and Kyema G., WA)**

"I'm a very fortunate limited partner with Sterling Rhino Capital. The awesome thing about multifamily investing is that if you continue to do it, your money will grow like very little else I have ever found. I will definitely invest with Sterling Rhino again." **(Suzanne C., GA)**

"As a relative newcomer to real estate investing, I was looking for someone that I felt comfortable with as well as being trustworthy. Chris fit the bill on all counts. He has been very patient with my inexperience and has always been a phone call away for any of my concerns. When I had a problem with my bank receiving distributions, Chris took it upon himself to contact them and clear up the confusion. If you are considering investing in real estate, I strongly suggest that you consider Chris Roberts and Sterling Rhino Capital." **(Todd F., LA)**

I know when I was researching investing passively for the first time, referrals played a role in making my decision. You might even ask the referral if they know anyone else that has invested with the group you are vetting and see if you can get in touch with them as well.

Chapter 5
Raising Capital for Your First Deal

In the last chapter, I outlined how some of the multifamily influencers add value though their thought leadership platforms and shared examples of what investors will say about you if you deliver on your promise and communicate on a regular basis. Now I will give you some tips on how to raise capital with your thought leadership platform. Depending on your raise structure, fund or direct syndication, you might start raising money before you have your first deal under contract. (More about funds later.) This example below assumes you are building a base before you first deal is under contract.

Starting Your Marketing Campaign

In order to measure how effective your content is, you need to have a good CRM as outlined earlier in this book. Once you have this set up, you can track whether the content you are sharing is resonating so you can build off that success. Whatever is not gaining traction, you toss out or stop focusing on. Here is an example:

You run a social media post about multifamily investing and tie it to your CRM through plug-ins that track who is clicking and reading it. If they sign up to learn more or join your investor club, you might have a winner. Now that they have signed up, you track how much of your regular content being sent from your CRM is being read or shared. If people are clicking on your ads but not signing up, then you may want to change the messaging. The goal here is to get people into your closed loop of communication CRM so you can build a relationship with them. This will also be important when you manage distributions later after they invest, and you begin distributions.

Once these prospective investors come into your CRM through your marketing, you will need some kind of follow-up email or automation to keep them engaged. You can do this through sites mentioned earlier like Active Campaign, Mail Chimp, or others, but you must track and measure the engagement of your marketing and communicate with them on a regular basis once they have shown interest.

Phone Calls to Establish a Substantive Relationship

Once you have a prospect in your CRM, you want to offer a calendar link in your automations or in your email correspondence so they can get to know you, and you can qualify if you think it's a good fit for both of you.

On that call you will ask simple questions like these:

- What are your goals?
- How did you hear about us?
- Have you ever invested before?

- Are you an accredited or nonaccredited investor? (Or ask if they know the difference between the two.)
- When are you looking to invest?

You can drive interest to your CRM through hosting a podcast, running YouTube videos, Facebook, Instagram ads, or pay-per-click Google Ad words, but there is no substitute for word of mouth and referrals from your existing base once you get started.

Six Basic Principles when Engaging Potential Investors

Using some of these basics, we raised over $40 million and purchased over $150 million in asset in about a three-year period. Of course, you will expand your content and the frequency when you run to scale, but the basic principles are simple:

- Tell everyone that you are in the real estate investing space and explain what you do.
- Get very active in sharing content on social sites and via email.
- Have a system to measure your content and the responses from prospects.
- Take care of the clients coming into your ecosystem once you have earned their trust.
- Over-deliver on your promise and constantly communicate.
- Ask them to share their experience with others.

Now on to your first deal!

Chapter 6
A Class-C Property May Be a Good Place to Start

After you've established your brand identity and online market presence and have an idea of how much money you can raise, you can start searching for your first multifamily property! As a new investor, class-C multifamily properties, or properties in working class neighborhoods that need some renovation, offer many benefits such as the following:

- **Lower Acquisition Cost**. Class-C properties are less costly to buy than class-A or B properties, which gives you more opportunity to find something in your price range.
- **Bridge Debt Mortgages**. Usually, in working-class, value-add properties, you will use this type of debt for your loan. You may pay a slightly higher interest rate, but you will be able to finance up to 100% of the CapEx budget in the loan, allowing you to easily execute your renovations and lower the amount you need to raise from investors.
- **Cash Flow**. Class-C properties are considered riskier and therefore could have higher cap rates. Because of the low acquisition cost and ability to raise rents through the renovation or value-add

process, the property usually easily passes the 1% rule (the monthly rent needs to be close to 1% of the acquisition cost per unit—some call this "cost per door"), especially in the future pro forma projections. Therefore, the cash flow could be higher once the property is stabilized, as long as it's bought right. Here is a 1% rule example: A purchase price of $7 million, with a door count of 120, equals a purchase price of $58,333 per door. If the current rents are within the 6% to 10% range above or below $583 per month, then this could be worth further review. This is just a guideline and one of the dozens of tools you should consider in your first-glance underwriting. Now the 1% rule is used a lot in single-family home purchase analysis, but it could be used as a rough guideline in multifamily building purchases as well.

- **Deep Renter Pool**. Homeownership is usually a big challenge for this tenant base, so the pool of renters is a deep one.
- **Massive Opportunity for Forced Appreciation**. Because these properties need work and are acquired at lower costs, they have a huge potential for renovations and upgrades. They also usually have management issues and therefore present opportunities to decrease expenses and find new sources of income. With upgrades comes the opportunity to bring rents to fair market value. Combining increased revenue with operational efficiencies increases profits, which forces the appreciation or value of the property. Commercial real estate's value is, in part, based on the profitability of the "business." A class-A property, on the other hand, doesn't have much room for improvement and therefore can have a

little less upside potential at least from a value-add perspective. The exception to class A would be new development or ground-up construction.

- **An Excellent Learning Experience**. Renovating and managing a class-C property can be a major learning experience for you. To think that you're going to waltz into the commercial multifamily investing business, taking down class-A and B properties is a pipe dream unless you've teamed up with someone who already has that capability, and you ride their coattails. I see starting your journey with the rougher class-C properties as paying your dues or earning your stripes. When selecting a property, you're looking at the location, property condition or age, price per door, the income level of the tenants, and the condition of the property. Those are the four main factors when you're looking at a classification of a property. You should start by figuring out how much money you can raise. This will help determine the size and price of the property you can buy. There are generally five classes of property—new development, A, B, C, and D—that you come across. Class D could be older than thirty-five years or very rough around the edges or in some of the most challenged neighborhoods. They could also be listed in a fringe category like mobile homes and RV parks. Your average rent could range from $300 to $550 per month, but in some markets, even higher. With class C, you're generally going to be in an older area. You're going to have a higher crime rate. Generally, the property itself is going to be older, twenty-five to thirty-five years old in many cases. The income of the residents is generally going to be a little bit lower to middle compared to the national averages. So your average household income or individual income could be between $25,000 and, say, $45,000 versus the national average being between $55,000 and $60,000 or so, which would start getting you up into a class-B property.

Also, your property condition is going to have a lot of deferred maintenance. So these properties are good to get into because there's an opportunity to fix them up and then raise the rents, bringing up the value of the property through bringing up those rents. So a class-C property is generally going to be what we consider a value-add play with a little bit more challenged market and sometimes even a challenging tenant base, with lower average household income compared to the rents that you're trying to get to. Always consider your rent levels—how much rent you might charge, compared to a new development complex, whether it's class A, B, or C. In general, we don't see a lot of D. Class D might be considered mobile home parks or extremely heavy value-add massively deferred maintenance type of properties. Your C properties are going to come in somewhere around the $550 to $850-a-month rent range, and your Bs are going to be around $850 to $1,350 in rent. Your As are going to be somewhere around the $1,350-a-month-plus in rent. Class A rents may range from $1,350 to $1,950 or higher based on the markets they're in, and new development could range from $1,950 to $3,350 or higher. We will dig into new development a bit later.

There are new development opportunities and class A, B, C, and D properties pretty much in every metropolitan statistical area (MSA) in each state. So you really are looking mainly for owner-operators. You're looking for noninstitutional-type properties because there is a good chance that they have not been renovated yet. You're looking for generally a little bit lower price point. Because of that, your C and D properties are going to start out at a lower price point, let's say, in the lower millions, the single-digit millions, a price point range from $2 to $6 million or so. You could be looking at opportunity zones. Those are zones deemed by governments to have tax incentives for growth. These can be great areas to develop a new multifamily apartment complex because of the tax incentives. Up to a 15% exemption on capital gains could be realized in some cases when investing in these areas of town, which can be passed on to investors. The city or town will define areas with run-down buildings or areas where they want to stimulate growth, and they'll provide incentives to buyers and investors to come in and fix those properties up or develop. The bottom line is you can get out and drive around, or you can do it on the internet, but you just need to do a lot of research and start talking to brokers. Ask them to send you those types of properties, if that's the type of property or area of development you want to invest in.

There's always a risk when you're investing or starting a business or buying a property. I would say that with these types of properties, the risk is your tenant base. Sometimes, you may have higher crime in an area. That's usually going to cost you a bit more on your insurance. Sometimes, your lenders won't want to lend. It just depends on the type of debt you're trying to get. Or you might pay a premium on your debt. It's typically going to be a little bit tougher to turn those tenants over and reoccupy the building with tenants who follow the new rules while cultivating a better, more family-friendly environment.

Bad debt could be an issue as well. So you want to make sure that you're putting enough money in reserve to handle the potential bad debt when you come in and try to turn that property around. Bad debt can occur when you have to evict people. It takes time, so bad debt could be people that might not pay their rent on time or people that are just protesting because they're angry. They like living in a slumlord condition, which you obviously don't want. You want to fix the place up so kids can go out and play and feel safe while helping turn the neighborhood around. So those are some of the things you have to be ready for—all the challenges that come with the type of tenant base and the environment that you're going into.

To handle these types of issues, preparation is crucial. It's like anything else. You have to think ahead and put a plan in place. You can raise enough money to offset the challenges that you're going to have. You may lower the returns for your investors, but they know that going in. Often, with a class-C property, you may not have as much cash flow in the beginning for your investors, because you have to renovate, rid the building of crime, and do all these things. But the payout at the end can be great, sometimes significantly higher than other asset classes, because the upside is so great. In many cases, you're buying them at a lower price point because there's so much deferred maintenance. So I would say just prepare on the front end and be ready for all the potential issues—the deferred maintenance, the crime, and the bad debt. Make sure you do your research. I would encourage you to meet with the city council and the sheriff or the police chief and just understand what you're getting into before you take a deep dive.

The next chapter will tell you what to look for in a strong negotiator.

Chapter 7
Who Should Negotiate?

When it comes to successful negotiation, it is so much more than just two people meeting, stating their terms, and strong-arming their opponent into submission. Negotiation is like a dance. The best negotiators understand the give and take of it and do it in a way that puts their opponent at ease instead of on the defense.

So if you're a syndicator or lead on a team, here are the important traits you should look for when choosing your negotiator for the due diligence process, especially if dealing directly with the seller:

1. **They have excellent people skills**. The best negotiators have excellent people skills and are able to sway people by relating to them. They actively employ customer service soft skills, such as empathy and active listening. They take time to make sure the opposition feels heard and respected, and they create custom solutions based on what they learned.
2. **They've done their homework on the opposition**. The person you select to negotiate should be able to do their homework and figure out who they are meeting with before the actual meeting. This means determining things like, "Are you buying from another syndicator, investment

group, or private seller?" and "Is the deal an on-market or an off-market pocket deal?"

3. **They stay calm under pressure**. Negotiations are inevitably a high-emotion experience on both sides of the deal, so it's very important to keep a cool head. This means staying emotionally detached from the outcome and not overreacting if the other side has an advantage or starts getting emotional or dramatic themselves.

4. **They understand both parties' goals**. The best negotiators to use are the people who have a clear understanding of both parties' goals and leverage it to close the deal. Understanding your own goals means making sure you know what the end goal of this deal is. Are you trying to get the property at the lowest price point?

Understanding the opposition's goals takes a little bit of work. It means asking the right kind of questions and listening to the answers so you can prepare the best terms, presentation, and approach that makes the opposition feel seen, heard, and valued. If you are buying from a syndicator or investment group, their motivations for selling may be strictly numbers-driven. If buying from a private seller, it could be more personal. It's important to dig in and figure out what is motivating this transaction. Here are some examples:

- A fellow syndicator may be selling so they can move on to a larger project as their asset has come to maturity; then they may hold firm on the numbers they need to achieve at exit as they work to hit pro forma.
- A private seller may have fallen into a hardship or suffered a recent loss and be motivated by the freedom of getting out of the asset or to liquidate

some equity. They may be willing to drop the price or make other concessions as a result.

When choosing your negotiator, consider how many factors go into the negotiation and how you will negotiate from a position of strength. The process can take a lot of back-end work and verbal judo, but if done correctly, the results can be amazing.

Now check out these five tips from Chris Voss on Masterclass. com

How to Negotiate: 5 Tips for Negotiating Better

A successful negotiation is one in which you, either as buyer or seller, achieve an outcome that feels equitable. Not everyone is born with innate negotiation skills. Fortunately, there are proven ways to become a good negotiator. Extensive research shows that certain negotiation tactics continually yield results in both remote and face-to-face bargaining.

Why Are Negotiation Skills Important?

Mastering a proven set of negotiation techniques can yield dividends over the course of your life. [17] In fact, strong negotiating skills can be among the most valuable assets a person can have. Throughout your life, the negotiation process may come into play for the following activities: buying and selling merchandise, overseeing real estate transactions, salary negotiation (from setting a starting salary to angling for a higher salary), assessing the market value of a good or service, and problem-solving in interpersonal dynamics, including conflict resolution.

1. **Make the first offer**. One of the best negotiating strategies is to seize control of the bargaining table. The best negotiators do this by setting the initial terms of a negotiation.

2. **When discussing money, use concrete numbers instead of a range**. If you're selling a piece of jewelry and you tell your buyer that you're looking to get between $500 to $750 for it, you're likely going to get the lower price.

3. **Only talk as much as you need to**. One of the shrewdest negotiation strategies is to harness the power of silence. In real life, silence can throw people off their game and affect their decision-making.

4. **Ask open-ended questions and listen carefully**. When you're trying to get your way, it rarely pays to ask simple yes or no questions. To make a back-and-forth dialogue work for you, ask open-ended questions that make the other party cede valuable information.

5. **Remember, the best-negotiated agreement lets both sides win**. Dealmakers who have a win-lose mindset tend to alienate partners and kill the chance for repeat business. But dealmakers who push for win-win outcomes—where both sides get something they want—can open a lot of doors down the road.

There are a number of books you can read to learn more about how to negotiate. There's a great book called *Pitch Anything* by Oren Klaff.[18] There's another book called *Never Split the Difference* by Chris Voss.[19] And there's another one called *The Secrets of Power Negotiating* by Roger Dawson.[20]

Chapter 8
Look for Hidden Issues (and Pay Close Attention to Obvious Ones Too!)

It is extremely important when putting an offer down on a property to make sure you fully understand what issues are present (and believe me, there are *always* issues). Making an offer without a clear understanding of the issues will not only cost you money but will also cost you time and energy trying to correct them. Let me give you an example of one of the multifamily properties we bought.

My team was presented an off-market deal on a class-C multifamily apartment complex with 112 units and an asking price of $5.2 million. Usually, properties that are up for sale come with a marketing package or at least a set of financials to review, but in this case, there were none. However, the email explained that the property was a "light" value-add, had very little deferred maintenance (which is great for a class-C property) and had only one owner since the complex was built nearly thirty years before.

Based on this, our group submitted a letter of intent (LOI), and after a little, negotiation we went under contract at $4.866 million. From the beginning, we ran into issues. It started with communication issues. The deal was sourced by a third-party referral, and several brokers were involved. Eventually, though, we were able to proceed with the transaction, and once the purchase and sale agreement (PSA) was signed, our team met to walk the property.

This is when we realized things were not as they were presented to us originally.

Maintenance and Repair Issues

Upon inspection, there was a ton of work that needed to be done. This was not a "light" value-add. On the outside, we could tell that multiple roofs needed replacement; driveways were badly damaged with potholes that could swallow a small child; there was a massive garbage problem; you could smell sewage from some of the building clean outs that were missing their covers; aluminum windows from the '80s that were not sealed properly; trees that had not been cut in thirty-five years; and roots that were lifting walkways over ten inches in some cases. Many other red flags stood out, just on the exterior. It became increasingly apparent that the complex was in very bad condition, and a lot of work would have to be done to make any money. This realization was coupled with the knowledge that the current condition was going to affect the underwriting significantly. But it didn't end there.

After seeing the state of the outside, my team began investigating other issues and found that the owner was in arrears with multiple local utility companies, and there were several unresolved code violations in place that, thankfully, due to a change in administration, were not being enforced. These were red flags, for sure, but they also presented an opportunity for us to determine what was going on and see if there was a way to leverage this information.

Too Many Hands in the Pot

After seeing the state of the property, my team began asking for specific documents to better understand the severity of the situation. Unfortunately, this proved to be a hard task. The seller recently had a significant change in her life and was in her later years. She started leaning on others to assist during the negotiation. So we were forced to work with her team, which included her own broker and eventually her son. Unfortunately, they had no prior experience with multifamily transactions.

So when we asked for things like the seller's financials, we were met with pushback. The brokers didn't understand why we needed bank statements, and the seller refused to share tenant leases. At least it felt like they did not know how important some form of formal documentation was. Since they were inexperienced with multifamily transactions, it felt like they didn't understand that documents such as a T-12 ("Trailing 12" is a financial statement for a multifamily property that shows the previous twelve months of operations) and rent roll are required by lenders. Without these documents, a buyer would not be able to get a loan on the property. I could have been wrong, but this really seemed unnecessary. One would think the brokers would have found a quicker solution.

This caused a lot of back and forth and heartache. There was a ton of work that went into the due diligence, and just as the deal felt like it was getting close, something else would come up that pushed it twice as far away.

Make Sure the Contract Fits the Situation

In addition to everything else, we realized that we had an inadequate contract for a deal as complicated as this one. When this opportunity was first presented to me, on the surface, it made sense. You see, the original contract stated that due diligence would not start until all the appropriate documents (ledgers, T-12, or a profit-and-loss report) were provided to the buyers. Under normal circumstances, you would have a deadline of ten to twenty days for these documents to be provided and the clock to start.

But because of what appeared to be a lack of experience of the brokers and cooperation by the sellers in providing any type of meaningful reports, the deal was not moving forward, and this went on for months.

As a new investor, it is imperative to make sure your contract fits the specific situation for the property you are purchasing. Blanket and generalized contracts just won't do when you're making a deal for an investment property such as this, because there are likely clauses in the contract that don't make sense, aren't applicable, and don't benefit or protect you. Make sure you know what you are getting into and have a good real estate–specific attorney draft the docs based on your due diligence.

So in our case, since our contract allowed the buyers to take their sweet time providing documentation before we started due diligence, we were at their mercy. Finally, after ten weeks of asking for them, the broker provided handwritten (yes, handwritten) ledgers of the rent records and a T-6 document, neither of which were even close to being adequate for a bank loan, complicating the issue even more.

When faced with hurdles such as these, many investors may decide that the property is not worth the risk and associated headache, and they will pull out of the deal. And that's exactly what happened.

One of the original partners decided after all these antics that he was pulling out of the deal, and his earnest money would need to be refunded. Even though it was a blow to the deal, it actually presented us with an opportunity to find a new partner and rewrite the contract to fit these specific and unique circumstances. So we jumped on it.

Once a new partner stepped in, we rewrote the contract, readied the new earnest money check, and started negotiations with the sellers once again.

Chapter 9
Don't Be Afraid to Hold Your Ground

As usual, after sending the new contract and asking for the property financials, the sellers dragged their feet. While most might see this as a negative, we took advantage of it by investigating and digging up as much information on the owners and property as we could to use as leverage points once the sellers agreed to begin negotiations.

Four months later, though, with no end in sight, we decided to put the ball in the seller's court, and we drew a line in the sand—we needed either the documents or a signed PSA, or we would walk.

Only a few days later, they were ready to play.

Presenting the Counteroffer

We began moving forward, going through due diligence, and completing all the required neighborhood work. But it quickly became even clearer that the asking price needed to come down. After the hassle of getting this far, most on the team had doubts the seller would be willing to come down on the price, but rather than give up, we presented a counteroffer of $3.6 million. This was less than the original offer of $4.866 million.

It is important when presenting any type of counteroffer to provide context to the broker for why the price is the way it is and why you consider it to be fair. Otherwise, the sellers will believe that you aren't playing fair. This is also known as a re-trade, and as a result, the seller may not be open to considering the offer. When you provide context, though, and present the facts, then the sellers have no choice but to come to the same conclusions you did, even if they don't like it.

So included with our counteroffer was a detailed breakdown of what we found, all the potential issues, and the estimated cost or potential loss as a result of those issues. Keep in mind, a sophisticated seller would likely know what they were selling and might not be as flexible, but in our case, we were dealing with a family member of the original owner whose only motivation was to get this over with because he did not want to be involved in the first place, but he was sticking with the price so far.

After presenting our counteroffer, the brokers informed us that there was another offer on the table (even though this was supposed to be an off-market deal). Sidenote: It's very rare to find an off-market deal. Off-market usually means it's just sent to a handful of people, but just know you're not the only one seeing it. Unfortunately, because it was an off-market deal—or we can call it an unlisted deal, with no records or offering memorandum/presentation deck—there really was no way to be sure if there was actually another offer. It could have been just a ploy by the sellers or brokers to get us to increase the offer price. So after the team convened and did a little digging, we concluded that if there was truly another offer, it was probably around $4.125 million, which meant we would need to do some negotiating in order to keep the deal going.

Renegotiating deals is a very delicate balance (especially when another offer is in play) and must be conducted with patience and tact. We knew the other offer (if there was one) was higher than our counteroffer, but since the other buyers had obviously not done the due diligence that we did, we believed it was very unlikely that this new group would work the sellers down to the low numbers we concluded after our initial due diligence.

On the flipside, though, if there *wasn't* actually another offer, and the sellers were motivated to sell, they would likely stick with us because they know after all this time it would close much faster. So the goal was to work our numbers and get as close as we could to our underwriting without blowing the whole deal up. On a sidenote, when you're dealing with one broker that represents the seller and buyer, which is typical, they will give guidance to the best of their ability and, in most cases, eliminate the guessing game. They will, however, work the buying side to get as much for their client as possible.

We decided to increase our offer to $4,012,500, which was lower than the alleged second party's offer and still well below our first negotiated price of $4,866,000. Our new price was actually 66% lower than the last agreed-upon price, so not a bad negotiation by any means if we could get it to stick. The new price of $4,012,500 was set, and the sellers agreed to it, saying that even though our offer was lower, they chose us because of the experience of our sponsor and our professional presence and credibility. They said they were confident that we could close the deal after we provided some of our net worth documents, showed our website, and provided proof of experience (this ties back to having an established brand identity and market presence).

Even though it took them five months to figure this out, it was worth it.

Pushback to Our Counteroffer

When we presented the counteroffer, we experienced pushback every step of the way, every time—particularly when we were negotiating with the brokers, both their broker and our broker. For whatever reason, things kept getting lost in translation. Of course, the selling broker was trying to fight to get the highest price for his client, but nobody wanted the deal to fall through. Our broker was doing everything he could to keep it from falling apart. So we had this back-and-forth thing going on, and then we had a seller with no experience in selling commercial property.

In other words, they hadn't sold multifamily apartments before. So you're trying to explain the market to them and what's going on, and then the brokers are pushing them, saying, "Well, we can always put it back on the market." But they didn't want to put it back on the market because we'd been negotiating for months. And the broker did not want to put together a presentation deck or an offering memorandum and do all the market analysis. That would have been a ton of work and time for a small, single broker. They needed to close this deal as badly as we wanted to buy it. What we needed was a direct line of communication to streamline things and build an efficient process. So that's really where the challenge came in—having too many cooks in the kitchen, too many people involved in the process. That's why we eventually ended up just dealing directly with the seller. Fortunately, the seller ended up telling the broker he wanted to deal with me directly. I had requested this, but it fell on deaf ears several times.

In creating a counteroffer, we basically broke down some of the costs—the extensive costs that would be needed to renovate the property. We broke down the type of debt that we could secure based on the current price. In other words, we would need to put down more money with the bank to get debt on a property like this because the income wasn't high enough. They weren't showing us that the property was worth what they were trying to get for it. We needed to make them understand throughout the process that it didn't matter what you want for the property, and it didn't matter what I wanted to pay for the property—we really need to figure out how we could come to a common ground where the bank would lend us the money to buy the property. That's what it boiled down to. The only way around this was if they had a cash buyer, but we were not, and the sellers did not seem to want to wait for one. So there's this back and forth. I did provide those details in emails and spreadsheets, and even through phone calls—at first through the brokers, then through his attorney, then eventually directly with the seller. That's when I flew in, and we started working together directly.

This whole deal was very challenging because we didn't really know who and what we were dealing with at all. At first, it was through the brokers, and we thought, *Okay, this is great, we're working with reasonable sellers that we've dealt with before.* This was our first larger multifamily asset, but I had gone through quite a few real estate transactions, so I understood the process. We were dealing with the brokers, then we realized the brokers weren't well-versed in the multifamily space.

Then we found out that they were dealing with the eighty-six-year-old owner. This was the wife of the original builder, who had passed away, and then the kids came in to help. They were kind of helping, then one son ended up taking over, and we ended up negotiating pretty much primarily with him. He did not understand commercial real estate, making it a challenge to get the deal done. It was difficult throughout. At one point, before the kids finally stepped in, we dealt with two different attorneys as go-betweens from the sellers to the brokers. The first original attorney literally quit in the middle of our deal, due to some strange conflict of interest. Ugh! Now, on to attorney number 2.

This was an atypical deal because, in most scenarios, you will deal directly with your broker. Our broker was communicating with another broker who represented the seller for this transaction. In most cases in commercial real estate, the commercial broker who represents the seller generally represents you as well. You can have your own broker, but that's not customary. Generally, the seller's broker just represents both of you, and you communicate through that person. In my case, we had two different brokers, for complicated reasons. I would have preferred not to have that, but we did. Not only did we have that, but we also had an eighty-six-year-old owner who was friends with the listing broker. Not that age matters, but she had no desire to deal with the sale or negotiate. Then she ended up handing it off to the son to help her with it. He was retired and in his sixties, with no real estate experience or really any desire to expedite the process. So there were way too many people involved. At times, it seemed as though they could care less if it sold.

Nevertheless, they finally accepted our counteroffer, and we were ready to move forward.

Chapter 10
Expect the Unexpected

Figure Out Your line, and Draw It in the Sand

If you remember, early in the negotiations, the sellers were unwilling to provide most of the required documents, including their insurance, T-12, rent rolls, utility bills, and more. Even though we wanted the property, at one point, it became clear that without the seller's participation, we weren't going to close this deal.

This is important for you as a new investor to understand. Sometimes, you just have to know when enough is enough and be willing to walk away. If you're not leading this deal, then you are quite literally at the seller's mercy, and you cannot negotiate from a position of strength unless you're leading.

So we had to say, enough is enough, and we drew a line in the sand. Either the sellers were going to provide the documents, or we were going to walk. It was a risky move, especially considering we really wanted the apartment complex, but it paid off. Within twenty minutes, we were given a document we had asked for repeatedly over a period of months. It was so strange. We could not figure out if they were just playing games or hiding something, or if this was just a jumbled mess because of all the people involved. It was just odd behavior.

That's when we realized that if we were going to close this deal, we were going to have to play the game. Things were looking up, and it finally appeared as though things were coming to a close.

But then the unthinkable happened and caused the entire deal to change.

After about ten days of going back and forth with the sellers, the entire country was hit with a global pandemic that basically shut down the world. Banks started going crazy. It was said that the economy was about to go into another recession, and the nation basically went into lockdown as a result of the COVID-19 virus spreading everywhere. Since we were smack-dab in the middle of a deal when this happened, we had to determine the following:

- What price could the deal work at now?
- What is the worst-case scenario in terms of lending?
- How will this change the amount of equity we are going to have to raise?
- How on earth are we going to do due diligence during a lockdown?
- What is this going to do to the tenant base and the income of the property?

We also had some new considerations:

- Rates were previously around 5.25% for bridge debt or 3.75% on a Fanny or Freddy loan.
  - In this scenario, you could underwrite a deal with maybe 20% to 25% down, a debt ratio of around 1.2, and basic reserves of around three months of debt or so.

- ○ But now, bridge debt is basically gone. On the rare occasion when you can find it, it's 6%. Fanny and Freddy jumped to 4.75%, 30% to 35% down, with a debt service coverage ratio (DSCR) from 1.35 and up. They also now require a minimum of twelve-month principal and interest in reserves and twelve months of expenses and/or tax and insurance in reserves.
- ○ This deal is more of a bridge debt deal, but we may not have a choice but to go agency at this point (meaning, debt provided by a federal government agency). The question is, can we even get agency debt on this? Yikes!

So what does this mean for our deal?

- For a deal of this magnitude, we needed at least an additional $225,000 to $325,000 in reserves from our investors.
- We now had to account for all the potential job losses and bad debt in our underwriting, things that weren't addressed a mere twenty-four hours ago.
- We went from assuming an average of maybe 5% to 7% vacancy and 5% bad debt, to 5% to 7% vacancy and 20% to 30% bad debt at a minimum. What!

When factoring in at least 4.50% Freddy debt, 5% vacancy, 20% bad debt, 30% down, no refinancing in the deal, and a twenty-five-year mortgage, this could literally wipe out 90% of the deals being underwritten, because the pain of this new reality would not be felt by the sellers for about four to eight weeks (sometime after the first and second rent collections). This meant we needed to renegotiate our future terms. So we decided to come in with a new offer of $3.6 million, which ironically was about what we wanted to pay before

COVID-19 hit, but we had moved up based on other offers and the fact that we could make it work pre-COVID-19 at the higher price.

To help further offset the costs, we changed our initial plan of a full $1-million rehab with an aggressive rent escalation through Year Four, down to a small clean-up budget of $250,000, and we adjusted to a very conservative slow roll on rent escalation. This made a big difference, believe it or not.

This new underwriting model was a perfect fit in this instance, because it was a class-C multifamily apartment complex and run by an owner operator for thirty-plus years, the rents were the lowest in the market by far, and they were at 100% occupancy (this was a big benefit to this type of property).

We knew that while there would still be bad debt, it was likely to get paid eventually, and due to the low rent, tenants would be more inclined to stay based on the market conditions, even with an increase in rent. In other words, the rents were so low, if you couple it with this low purchase price, we could just raise rent without a significant renovation budget, and the deal would still yield higher-than-average returns at a sale.

Chapter 11
Look for Opportunities to Reduce Costs

After almost six months of negotiation, I thought we had it, but the sellers (of course!) countered at $4 million. This was only $12,500 lower than where we were before countering at $3.6 million. While the amount was minuscule in the grand scheme of things, I knew I needed to be firm and stand my ground or walk away. I drew a line in the sand at $3.8 million, and after a week, they decided to pass on my offer.

I let it sit for a while and found out that the buyer from a few months before was back in the picture, so the broker said, but apparently, they were asking the sellers for things I knew they would not provide. I also knew the sellers would not want to start over with this group, so I figured the best thing to do was to see if the seller was open to renegotiating the deal. I presented my version of a win-win offer. By this time, the interest rate had dropped slightly to 4.2%, and a couple of other options were loosening up, including the banks lowering their reserves required from twelve to eighteen months down to about six months.

Potential Savings: Affordable Housing

While I waited to hear back from the sellers, I also explored twelve-month tax breaks and asked the lender if we would qualify as an affordable housing building. "Affordable housing" is defined as an apartment complex with rents at 80% or below the median average in the area. These rents at purchase price were only $550 per month, well below the market average. This is not the same as HUD or Section 8 low-income housing. This is just if your rents are lower than market averages by 20%.

Qualifying as affordable housing was a Fanny-Freddy lender opportunity, and if we qualified, we could drop our rate even further. By reworking the underwriting, I could still hold my conservative position to protect my investors, and this deal would still pencil nicely. This new assessment put me in a position to move up slightly on my all-or-nothing price of $3.8 million.

Use Vacancy and Bad Debt to Renegotiate

After I knew I had some wiggle room to make this deal, I reached out to the sellers to explain my reasoning for the $3.8 million price I offered. Doing this allowed the seller to better understand my concerns. In this case, I explained that there were too many unknowns surrounding the amount of bad debt and vacancy in the next few months, especially considering the handwritten rental logs and the fact that I basically had to rely on his word versus a property management company's record, which would have been customary. I further explained that while the complex is at 100% occupancy for now, my team was anticipating a significant drop in the future as a result of the pandemic and its unknown effect on the economy.

I stated that if the sellers could provide occupancy and bad debt above 95% the month before closing, I would pay $3.9 million, but if it was below that, then I would get a $100,000 credit closing at my offer price of $3.8 million. They understood but felt they were being unfairly penalized because if just a few units went vacant or had bad debt, they would be hit with a $100,000 charge.

So we came up with a compromise. I called it the "COVID Clause":

- The last complete month before closing, if the unit vacancy fell below 106 of the 112 units (about 5% of the units), or if there were any units with a late or bad debt of more than two weeks, it would result in me getting a credit of $6,500. We calculated this figure by taking the amount of rent ($550) and multiplying it by twelve months.
- I had underwritten a vacancy and bad debt factor of 25% at the current average rent of $550 per unit, so this deal would break even at 22 units being evicted (bad debt) or vacant. Anything between 84 and 112 units would be a profit. So for every unit under 106, we would have a buffer, as though they were occupied for an additional twelve months. This is like having twelve months of reserves on each unit that does not perform.

After explaining it to the seller, the seller decided to take the $3.875 million price without the concessions clause for vacancies and bad debt. Great! Now we could get the contract revised and start rocking and rolling, right?

Chapter 12
Get Everything in Writing

It is important when negotiating new offers to make sure you get them in writing as soon as possible. Doing so will save you a ton of extra work and headaches in the long term.

So after lengthy negotiations with the seller of our multifamily apartment complex, we finally came to an agreement. But two weeks later, as I waited for the seller's attorney to send over the revised PSA, our broker called to tell me the seller forgot all the details we had discussed and was confused, meaning we now had to renegotiate the terms—again!

After renegotiating, we finally settled on $3,300 for any unit past twelve-unit vacancies or twelve units with late payments past two weeks. This would be measured the last month before closing, and we had a final purchase price of $3.9 million. We were both happy with the result and had eliminated what were sure to be two more attorney interactions and who knows how many more broker calls.

With this new rate and lenders opening a bit, we could now underwrite three options:

- The conservative clean-up and stabilize approach, with very low capital.
- Renovate each unit for around $2,700 per unit and clean up the exterior with a rebrand.
- Full renovation of each unit for $6,500 per unit with a $1-million budget, including some exterior work.

There was so much back and forth and confusion at this point that I not only ended up on the phone with the seller's attorney, but the seller also called me, and he and I began working out the rest of the details without the brokers. During the call, I explained why it was so critical to get at least four months of consistent recent income to reflect an occupancy of over 90%. After a bit of give and take, the seller finally provided the reason they were so adamant about not providing the financials to us.

The actual owner (we can call her Momma Bear) stated two things when she started the process of selling the complex:

- She didn't want to pay the closing costs.
- She didn't want to provide the financials until *after* we signed the PSA.

These two small details were never discussed with us and were the main things holding up the deal. Once I understood this, we were able to find a compromise. The twelve-month income was finally sent to me after an audit, but only by text message, and the sellers gave their word that the numbers were accurate. With these initial numbers, we had what we needed to proceed, and knew that as soon as we signed the PSA, we would have access to all the documents to confirm their findings.

With due diligence, we had a seventy-five-day window to pull out of the deal with 100% of the earnest money being returned for any reason, so we were protected in case the documents were inaccurate or insufficient for the lenders.

So finally, seven months after the original discovery of this deal, through partners changing, conditions changing, the deal falling out of contract for four months, and then back to the table for more negotiations, we were ready to sign the PSA. Our patience paid off, because we negotiated a very good discount for our investors, and the sellers were happy because they had confidence that we could close the deal now that we had built a relationship directly with them.

PSA Timelines

Generally, when you sign a PSA, everything is outlined: Seller has to provide this; buyer has to provide that; you have thirty days to do this or do that. I had negotiated an extended timeline because after you get past a certain timeline, your money is forfeited if you walk away. We needed the extension because they didn't have the documents that we thought they had. The brokers kept asking for them, but the brokers never actually met with the sellers to specifically explain what we needed and ask them, "Do you even know what these documents are?" And the reality was, months and months and months down the road, I finally did that and found out they didn't even know what the brokers were asking for. It just wasted so much time. You can make a deal happen without really detailed financials, but it's much more difficult and costly, and it's much easier if you have all that stuff up front. This was a very unique deal, and we learned a lot through the process.

When you're negotiating upfront timelines, the thirty days for due diligence is a time where, if you see something catastrophic on the property, you can go back and renegotiate it. They call that a re-trade. I don't recommend doing that. You should know what the potential issues are before you sign your contract. Because you can go in ahead of time before you sign a contract or at least get a feel for it on your property tour. After thirty days or so, generally, you're in that deal. I recommend you also try to bring along a property management company rep and contractor on you tour. You're going to lose your risk capital that you've put up if you try to walk away, but in some cases, our money is hard or nonrefundable from Day One. If that is the agreement, you better do a lot of digging on your tour.

So, let's say, you put up $200,000. After that first thirty days, if you don't find any reason to walk away, your money goes to that seller now, and you're in. You're moving forward no matter what, whether you can secure financing or not. It's rare that a seller will let you put in a finance contingency, meaning that if you can't secure financing, you can get your money back. If you don't know this already, while you will have a term sheet and tentative approval from your lender, that is not a guarantee you will get funded for your project. Getting the final approval can literally run right up to weeks before you are slated to close. I know this sounds crazy, but that's the way lending works, and it's because it takes months for lenders to qualify the asset you are buying and qualify you as a buyer. The more info you have ready for them and the more efficient you are, the better your chances for approval.

It's important to try to negotiate as much time as you can in the beginning to do that review period. I negotiated seventy-five days total in this process. Now, that's generally unheard of. That's a long time. So you've got thirty days, and then, usually, another thirty if you're lucky. We negotiated another fifteen on top of that, but a lot of this was tied to them not providing the right documents, the ones we needed to secure financing. So we weren't going to risk getting back our money and losing it when they weren't providing things they needed to provide. So that allowed us to just sign an agreement and extend. To extend, sometimes you've got to put a little more money down. But that's how we got seventy-five days. Generally, you would get thirty to forty-five days. We worked really hard to get something a lot longer, and I highly recommend getting as much time as you can to not lose your money early on in the process.

Sh*t Happens

As we were grinding along on due diligence, the seller casually mentioned that there was a fire in one of the units, and when I pressed for more information, he stated that while they were not aware of the full extent of the damage, they *did* know it was caused by a child putting fireworks in the HVAC unit. What?!

In addition, they disclosed that the tenant had not paid rent in three months.

Here's the problem with this news: We went under contract with no insurance claims on record, which helped keep our rates down, but we now had a tenant that was already behind and had moved out, making it a lender issue, and creating the risk for insurance rates to change when we finalized the insurance provider.

While not an immediate issue, we knew it might become one once we got closer to closing, as there may need to be concessions, and the lender was sure to impose very specific remedy standards for closing. We were then notified that the lender's inspection and appraisal had been scheduled.

Important note: In preparation for the lender's inspection, it is extremely important to prep the seller. Make sure the seller knows to keep things straightforward and professional with the lender and instruct them to not volunteer more information than is necessary and cooperate with any request if they can.

Even though we prepped our seller, they made a few mistakes in the actual numbers reporting (which had to be explained) and would not let the lender in to inspect the fire-damaged unit, citing "the fire marshal told me not to let anyone in."

After following up with the owner and explaining that the lenders needed access, the next day (miraculously!), the seller stated he was given the OK to enter and the lenders were welcome to come back. This is a bit of insight as to the type of seller I was dealing with—are you starting to see the picture? They rescheduled a second visit to bring the team back, specifically for this fire-damaged unit, but not before sending a slew of questions and requests for documents like the fire inspection reports and contractor quotes. They also wanted multiple photos of the unit, and they wanted them *before* they came back out.

Learning Opportunity: Everyone has their own systems, processes, and ways of doing things, but it is important that both you and the seller cooperate 100% with the lenders in every way and provide all requested info in a timely manner, while keeping in mind that in some cases, less is more. Provide exactly what they asked for, nothing more, because overdoing it may create more questions. Your lender-broker will guide you through this process, and a good one is worth their weight in gold. This is not the seller listing broker but a lender-broker that only represents you, the buyer. They are your connection to lenders you are trying to borrow from. I personally recommend using a good broker versus going directly to a bank or credit union, but in some cases, that can work out if you have an existing relationship.

Finally, we heard some good news. The fire damage was not extensive and did not displace any other tenants. The lender's appraisal came back only $500,000 higher than the purchase price, and the lender had no major issues with the inspection.

There were, however, a few items we needed to remedy before closing:

- We needed to get GFCI (ground fault circuit interrupter) outlets installed where outlets were within six feet of water, such as in bathrooms and kitchens.
- We also needed to purchase carbon monoxide detectors and have them installed in every unit.

As I planned my third trip to the property before closing, I knew I needed to review approximately ninety-five units for a quick visual and GFCI confirmation to finalize due diligence. I needed to meet with the property manager, and I also needed to meet with the locals, police commander, and CPA.

I also wanted to comp the lowest-priced apartment complex in the area to confirm our pro forma numbers are still in line from the revised underwriting (remember we are in the middle of the COVID-19 pandemic).

When you're dealing with subcontractors, vendors, and other partners associated with your deal, it's important to outline your business dealings with contracts. During my last few visits, we secured several contracts and new vendors.

Below, Yauhen Zaremba of PandaDoc explains why contracts are important:[21]

> All businesses carry out transactions, from hiring employees and scheduling contractors to forming partnerships and seeking financial backing.
>
> But is it always necessary to formalize things with a written contract?
>
> Let's look at the purpose of a contract and explore why contracts are important for establishing business relationships and protecting everyone's interests.
>
> **What is a contract?**
>
> A contract is a **legal agreement** that sets out the terms of a transaction, deal, or exchange between two or more parties—which may be individuals or companies.
>
> You might sign a contract to buy real estate, accept a job, or enter a business partnership. A **sales agreement** also counts as a contract.
>
> Contracts outline the **rights and responsibilities** of each party, as well as the costs, benefits, and details of how the contract may be terminated.

The purpose of a contract

The **purpose of a contract** is to establish and formalize a relationship by clearly defining the terms and obligations.

- **Identification**. The definition of all the parties to which the contract applies.
- **Offer**. The promise that one or both parties will (or will not, in the case of non-disclosure agreements) perform a specific action.
- **Consideration**. Where something of value is promised in exchange for the actions.
- **Acceptance**. An expression that both parties have agreed to the terms.
- **Awareness**. Proof (such as signatures) that both parties clearly understand and agree.
- **Capacity**. Each signatory has demonstrated the "legal capacity" to understand what they're signing.
- **Legality**. All contracts are subject to the laws of the jurisdiction under which they operate.

You may not need a contract on every little thing, but it's important to note that you should strive to get everything in writing or even recorded on a live Zoom call or some other video-recording software if the results of the conversation offline could have an impact on your deal or transaction.

Chapter 13
Use Your Time Wisely

Now that we had the sellers on our side, it was time to move on to the next step in the process: We needed to meet with the property manager to try and secure them as our management team and review all the handwritten financials and records the seller promised us.

We scheduled two days for this, with the intention of knocking out a few other tasks such as the physical inspection of a few units, meeting with the city and local law enforcement, and possibly the local bank while we were there.

Use your time wisely when scheduling events such as this, so you can maximize your productivity and efforts. For example, this is also a good time to start lining up a few of the items the bank may need from you to secure your debt for the property, such as the following:

- Final PSA when signed
- Organization chart of your team and structure
- All the general partners' (GP) financial statements
- All the GPs' resumes or brief biographies
- GPs' rent owned schedules

At this point, we had spent a lot of time on the initial, or first pre–due diligence, on things like these:

- Roof review
- Initial title review (we did this a little early, but there was a reason)
- Fully inspected one unit with a contractor
- Renovation outline plan A
- Spoke with a few contractors that previously worked on the property
- Lay of the land from the city, local law enforcement, and utility companies
- Spoke to several property managers in the area about the property
- Spent a weekend parked in the parking lot at night to see what happens in the area
- Spoke with a few tenants in the area as a secret shopper
- Shopped ten to twelve-other comparable apartment buildings in the market

After the two-day due diligence period and a thumbs-up from the property management company, we felt pretty good about moving forward. But we still needed to secure the debt beyond a verbal agreement (get a solid rate sheet) and confirm the financials.

Now some opportunities that come your way are presented in a pretty little package. You may know the names of the big players in this area: CBRE, Marcus & Millichap, or Cushman Wakefield will have a sales deck that is a hundred slides deep, with incredible financials and pro formas, and literally so well written that you could use 70% of it for your investor presentation (after you verify the info, of course!).

Our deal was *not* that type of opportunity. Honestly, I would have written a $10,000 check to have something like that in my hand, had it been available, once I was a bit deeper into this deal.

Knowing this, you may be asking yourself: Why did I take it in the first place without that info? Why would I waste my time?

Well, I felt from the very beginning that what I was presented had value and the price they were asking for it could be negotiated. I felt there was a great deal in this opportunity if only I could carve it out of the rough block of stone that was sitting in front of me. It wasn't easy, but it could be done. In fact, several times throughout this deal I was told or experienced the following comments:

- You cannot get the price down. (I did.)
- There are no more negotiations. (I made them.)
- Why waste your time? (I didn't. I made over $1,000 per hour on this deal when we sold.)
- This is too much, and you should just walk away. (This was crazy, and I stayed in it, leaning in and up.)
- I'm done. (Not me, I never quit.)
- I'm moving on. (Good, we don't need quitters.)
- I will not do your work for you. (They ended up doing it anyway—I got what I needed by being tenacious, professional, and personable.)
- I'm not saying I will, but I will think about it. (They did what I needed.)
- You're not getting that. (I did get it.)
- There is no way they will do that. (They did it.)

Many people would say that these were deal breakers, but I always felt that these were opportunities to build the best deal ever. I knew that if I could maximize the skills of my team and build a really good story, we would make this happen.

Think of it this way: You are not just telling your story to the lender but also to the sellers, your investors, and everyone who will listen. This includes contractors, utility companies, property managers, law enforcement, city council, and many, many more, but you must stay positive and keep the end in mind without wavering. Stick to your principles and use the data and numbers to drive most of your decisions rather than letting the naysayers or your emotions drive them.

Stick to Your Timeline

When you have a project that comes up, let's say, you're buying a property, and you need a digital timeline out in front of you that everyone can follow. So I recommend, whether it's a spreadsheet or sort of an organizational software that's set up to assign roles and goals, somebody should be in charge of setting up the digital timeline so that you know: We have earnest money that's going up on January 1, and then that money goes hard and nonrefundable on January 30, and we have an inspection period. Then in the middle of all of that, you're trying to secure your funding. Let's say, by January 15, which is in between the time that that earnest money goes up and then goes hard, which is nonrefundable, you've got to be securing your lender. So you've already been given a preliminary sort of approval, but now you're working through it with the lender.

So these are just a few examples of some of the things you need to be thinking about. But in your timeline, there might be twenty-five line items over a 90 to 120-day period that are really important that need to be executed along the way. Some of these time-sensitive requests may be outlined by your real estate attorney, but you should have your own that are shared with the team on a regular basis.

During my second to last trip, I had a specific agenda for the thirty-six hours I was going to be at the property:

1. Inspect the units that we had not gotten the chance to see (approximately ninety) at the bare minimum, but attempt to get into all units while doing a broker, property manager, and buyer walk.
2. List any potential areas of concern not previously found, including a visual inspection of the unit that caught fire during the review period.
3. Review rent collections and any dispossessory filings that were outstanding (a dispossessory is what the county called the court filings for evictions).
4. Inspect and address any issues previously noted on the last visit, like a few sewer problems that needed to be addressed.
5. Meet with the city managers and law enforcement.
6. Meet with the CPA to outline a plan and collaboration with the future property managers.
7. Comp shop the lowest priced comp to see how it compares to previous underwriting and if there have been any adjustments as a result of the pandemic.

There was a lot to do here, so it was extremely important to be organized and focused on the timelines to ensure we got everything done. You could use software like Monday.com or ClickUp™.com for team collaboration. Knowing this, though, plan for things to unexpectedly come up and build some buffer time into the trip for them.

Day One

When I arrived, the day started with the seller being thirty minutes late. We had to gear up with face masks, face shields, gloves and basically hazmat suits just as an extra precaution while entering the units during COVID-19. It was around ninety-four degrees, with about 85% humidity, and a bit scary with the virus in the back of our minds, but we knew the inspections absolutely had to get done. We made the decision to purchase and install twelve carbon monoxide detectors to comply with the lender's minimum requirement and avoid a back and forth with the seller as the lender actually required the seller to install the devices but they would not. We were going to purchase the other one hundred detectors and have them installed before closing but wanted to get some up during the visit.

During the inspection, we were notified of the following:

- There were around six units that had reported COVID-19 cases, so we could not enter those units.
- There were at least fifteen units with animals, but only two leases had pet fees being charged.
- There were at least nine units with a leak from the upstairs bathroom into the living rooms (a few of them were half-repaired, we assumed by a non-licensed repair man), and three upstairs bedroom ceilings with slight ceiling leaks.
- There were a handful of toilet or kitchen sink leaks and several units with deferred maintenance issues.

Thankfully, we had negotiated at least $100k during our original back and forth, knowing we would come across a lot of these issues. Surprisingly, there were no signs of insect or termite damage.

I met with the owner after six hours of unit inspections to review what I found and discuss the previous sewer issues.

After questioning the seller on several plumbing, but specifically sewer line, issues, I found out that there was a third plumber that was not disclosed during my last visit and who had been working on some of the issues.

This was a good thing because I was under the impression that the seller was avoiding my concerns based on his responses to emails. I asked for copies of all the invoices so I could review the scope of the work, and after tracking down the plumber's contact info, I was able to clarify several points of contention and put my mind at ease. We agreed to think things over and discuss it again in the morning.

Day Two

I started the next day by meeting with the city official to discuss our plans for the property and review how we could partner with them to make the community and building a better place to live. He felt the meeting went so well he suggested I present what he and I discussed to the city council at a later date. They were very excited to have us take over the building and felt that the previous owners did not do much to collaborate or cooperate with them in any way.

I then comp shopped. Again, I wanted to see and confirm if much had changed since my last visit. I gathered additional intel on several other buildings that were at a higher price than our lowest comp. Next, I met with the seller to negotiate some of the issues, and after a back and forth and a little heat in our conversation, we settled on one more new roof and

$4,000 off the price, bringing the total discount value to $10,400.

While it was a bit challenging at times, I accomplished all of the line items and then some during the quick visit. Next, I got ready for the final stretch.

Back home, I began cleaning up the numbers and building the final packet to send to the lender brokers. I reached back out to the seller and mentioned that if he did not want to discount the $4,000 off the sale price, he could replace two roofs instead of one. After a few days, he agreed to replace two roofs with no discount, which was great because this was another $2,600 discount from our last negotiation.

As we approached the closing date, the late payment and vacancy clause I added to the PSA paid off. I'm not sure if it was the COVID effect, the lack of filing evictions until June, or the sellers getting a little relaxed on collections, but the result was a $25,000 discount. Nice!

At this point, it appeared that our underwriting and closing costs were within about $10,000 of our original projections, which was great news.

Important Note: Always be conservative in your underwriting. You are far better off overestimating the numbers because you can recover by overcompensating. But by underestimating, you could literally break your opportunity in half and lose not only the deal but possibly some money as well.

Chapter 14
Know Your Numbers

If you can imagine for a moment not having a profit-and-loss report, no bank statements, T-12, or formal rent rolls, you can start to get a picture of the hassle I knew I was about to embark on. But that was just the beginning. The sellers had always stated from the beginning that the building was fully occupied, and I verified some of that on my visits, but when dealing with lenders and banks, they don't want hearsay—they want certified and organized documents. So here we go!

I spent days gathering and scanning hundreds and hundreds of manually written documents, which included the following:

- Receipt log sheets
- Applications
- Tenant logs
- Leases

All of these were handwritten using systems that were designed and employed when the building was originally built by the owners in 1983. Yes, you heard me correctly: 1983! Everything was handwritten by three different people, and in some cases, only using sticky notes for reminders and partial payments. I am not kidding. There were literally hundreds of colored sticky notes among the hundreds of photos of previous tenants that blanketed the dingy yellow 1983 wallpaper in the office. There were files and folders everywhere—it looked like a tornado hit a pile of documents that could have filled a Costco. It was crazy.

Even though it was a manual system, they did keep very good records. The problem was just that there were a lot of them, and they weren't all kept in one place. They needed to be confirmed, cross-referenced, and certified by the sellers. My challenge was they did not know how to do any of this, so I had to teach them and had to eventually walk them through all of it in person on multiple trips.

One of the requirements I put on the seller for me to sign the PSA, fly out, and review these documents was that they needed to provide me with proof that there was enough income in the last ninety days to justify the purchase. By the time I left the property to fly home, I verified that the numbers provided to me were wrong and were being calculated on a monthly deposit ratio versus the actual collections for the month collected.

Learning Opportunity: When you are verifying collections, make sure you are on the same page as the seller and 100% verify the actual collections multiple times so your numbers are correct for the bank. Don't believe anything unless you verify it yourself. Even if the intentions are good, you could be confirming apples to oranges, and the handwritten and manually calculated numbers could be off. Every little bit counts, so don't take even one collection for granted.

Even though the calculations were incorrect, I chose not to panic because I knew I only had part of the story, and I needed to spend a few days going through my hundreds and hundreds of scans and needed to build my own spreadsheets to paint the most accurate picture. Once completed, I could have the seller build his own from mine or at least verify and certify the data we built.

While I was doing this, one of our partners began the process of applying for lenders by shopping banks, credit unions, and Fannie and Freddie as well. Since this was going to be a value-add, bridge debt would be a good way to go so we could finance in the CapEx (capital expenditure, the money needed for repairs and improvements), but with the COVID-19 issues, rates and terms were not as favorable. The credit unions had some interesting terms, but again, not as good as what we were seeing with the agency debt. The only challenge in a post-COVID world was that the agency lenders were requiring substantial reserves of nine to eighteen months, which could reduce investor returns, even if, in most cases, we would get the funds back after nine to twelve months. I was not even sure if the agency would lend in this area as they can get pretty specific when selecting where they issue debt. Always check with your broker on the markets you are shopping in. If you are in a secondary or tertiary market, that may affect the type of debt you can get.

After gathering the last fourteen months of data, I quickly concluded there was a problem. The numbers were not only substantially different from what the seller had originally presented, but they were also inconsistent with the reported occupancy (remember, we were told the building had an occupancy of 98% to 100% and fairly low bad debt at the time of the due diligence visit, and had a reported historical vacancy of around 5% to 7%). Once I analyzed the data, it showed an "economic vacancy" (the number of vacant units plus delinquency of current tenants) of 15% to 20%.

This level of economic vacancy is unacceptable and will not secure favorable debt. There is no way you're getting agency debt with an economic vacancy above 15%, or a physical vacancy of more than 10%. At this point, we were beginning to shop agency a bit harder and were considering raising the extra money for CapEx versus drawing it from the bank so agency could work.

After this realization, I asked the seller several times if I had all the available data and was told yes. However, I remembered that there were some tenant log cards that were a backup for the rent receipt, and I wondered if maybe some of the missing rents were on the cards, even if they were missing from the receipt books.

All of this took me about a week or so to figure out something was off, because every time I would ask the seller about the numbers, they would tell me they collect almost all the rents, even though some tenants were slow to pay.

So I had to ask myself: "What am I missing?"

After going back and forth with the sellers and at least two weeks of painstaking data analysis, I realized there were two different receipt books being used. In addition, some of the collections from tenants and the subsequent receipts being given to them were also missing but were in the tenant logs.

These missing receipts or collections could only be found by running a weekly audit and requesting an explanation as to where the missing rents were. Once an explanation was given, I then needed to confirm them on the tenant log cards. If not for these tenant log cards, I would not have known there were two receipt books. The receipt book shared with me couldn't provide the whole story, and the one that was not being shared with me took a bit to figure out. We had applications, leases and confirmation that people were actually living in each unit, so we were okay, but this caused a tremendous amount of additional work. We found the existence of the second receipt book because the number sequence on the receipts would fall out of order and then get back in line. By taking months and months of rent collections and putting all the receipt numbers together, you could tell the seller was going back and forth with the two different books.

Now why would someone do that? Hmm. If he would have volunteered this, it would have saved a ton of time, but he never did. I only found out from our own research, and when I saw the extra receipt book on his desk, that was not part of the sequence. He was not being transparent, but why? This is going to get interesting. I know this is a bit confusing, but welcome to my world at the time. The bottom line is verifying and double-checking everything.

I had to reconcile fourteen months of data and hundreds, if not over a thousand, documents all over again so I could audit the entire process. I then highlighted the sheet sequences that were missing.

Learning Opportunity: It is so important that you have a full understanding of the financials because you may be questioned on the collection at some point. Always verify data with your own underwriting and cross-referencing regardless of how painful or time-consuming it is. You must do this as you are protecting everyone with your extra effort.

At the end of the day, my belief was that, based on the type of value-add, and the fact that the owners were original operators who built the property in the '80s, this would create a significant opportunity. I knew there was a lot of work to be done, but this could present a great opportunity. These are good indicators: when a property has a lot of deferred maintenance, when it's been the same owner/operator from the beginning, and when they're the ones selling it. And eventually, you deal directly with them. I knew that the price was slightly too high and that we just had to get the price down. Little did we know, with the way the economic trends were going, even if we had paid that price, we actually still would have delivered incredible returns for our investors. But getting the lower price actually helped even more. And based on the condition that the property was in, I knew we could capture a lot of upsides. I just knew that the return would far outweigh the headaches and challenges as long as I had the right team around me to execute the plan. I followed the data, and the data told me this deal would make a lot of sense.

Chapter 15
A Closed Mouth Won't Get Fed

Before my final flight out to pre-close, I sent the seller the list of items that were required by the lender before closing and a few things we as buyers wanted to discuss or negotiate.

Among my list were the following:

- We still needed to get the required GFCIs installed in the units (we found out later that we could have had them installed after the closing, but they had to be addressed and planned for before closing).
- The lender required the seller to install carbon monoxide detectors in each unit. For 112 detectors, we estimated the total cost to be $1,800 without labor.
- The lender required leases for twelve of the units they inspected to be pulled and reviewed (they wanted to verify the tenants' income averages, among other things). For 336 GFCIs, the cost would be anywhere from $2,500 to $15,000 with labor included.
- As the buyers, we listed a few sewer concerns, like a possible partial block on one line and a leaking fire hydrant that was listed as repaired but was not. We had also confirmed with the seller the

schedule of flushing one of the six sewer lines every six weeks to keep the lines free of debris. (Always confirm and get in writing all promised scheduled work. Someone's word is not as good as someone's work, but paper documentation and signatures are forever.)

The seller gave a lot of pushback on these things (as usual). Regarding the leases, the seller stated privacy laws prevented him from sharing them, and he wanted a letter from the lender explaining why that was necessary. He also refused to install the carbon monoxide detectors but did agree to address the GFCI issues.

This was great because with $15K of our money going toward our extension of the review period, and these requests being a lender requirement, we really had no choice but to handle them anyway. By staying on top of things, building rapport with the seller, and just asking for some assistance, we were getting somewhere and saved a little money in the process as well.

Chapter 16
Closing

As we prepared for the last visit before closing, there were a number of line items we needed to focus on. This included the following:

1. Meeting with the city leaders to discuss the property and outline where they could work with us to execute our plan. My goal was to figure out how we could partner together to improve the community, make an impact, and finalize our plan from previous visits with them.

2. Meeting with a few contractors, mainly our fence and security camera contractors.

3. Making copies of all tenant logs, obtaining a current rent roll, logging all rent deposits per tenant, reviewing rent collections, and making copies of any open work orders, including any parts that were on order, such as glass doors or appliances. My plan was to hold funds in escrow to fulfill any pending work orders or parts invoices.

4. Walking the property with the seller to highlight anything that needed to be removed in the office or on the premises by the day of closing.

Thankfully, the property management company found a good manager and was in the process of hiring a maintenance manager. We had a Zoom call before I left to outline the first sixty days of acquisition and work on the first things first list.

While we had a robust plan for the property, there were a few priorities.

Phase 1

Renovate the manager's building in the front of the property. We wanted to completely renovate the apartment above the office to test whether we could increase the rent to $750 for this unit, which happened to be our fifth-year pro forma number. So the plan was to renovate the manager's office, possibly convert what was a maintenance shop to four individual storage units that we could rent for $50 to $100 per space, and then rebrand the property and clean up the street sign. The total budget for this was between $22,000 to $27,000.

In addition, we wanted to work on our outstanding maintenance list and clean up the property. Next, we wanted to do a little landscaping. The total budget for this included $10,000 for landscaping, $15,000 for security cameras, and $25,000 to install a rear perimeter fence around the property.

Phase 2

During phase 2, our focus was on increasing rents on units with existing tenants while slightly increasing the rent on new units that were renovated to at least 20% above the existing tenants' new rent. Also, during this phase, we would start enforcing late payments and pet fees.

Phase 3

During phase 3, our focus was on reconditioning the driveway, replacing the roofs, and painting the exterior while continuing to slightly renovate units as they turn.

Last-Minute Issues

About a week away from closing, the lender-broker told us that the lender decided to take twelve months of our interest-only loan away for no reason. This was about $50,000 in cash flow in year two of our deal! I argued back and forth with the lender's broker but to no avail. They stuck to their guns. Unfortunately, that wasn't the end of the surprises.

About four days before the scheduled closing, we noticed on the lender letter that they also required an additional $90,000 in reserves for sixteen roofs that the engineer's report stated needed replacing. This was news to us, as we never saw an engineer's report.

My team was taken aback by all these blows to our already negotiated deal, so we got on the phone with the brokers and spent about thirty minutes negotiating a fix to this mess. After a few tense days, a 9:00-pm final call with the lender-brokers on a Saturday, and a few days extension on closing, we ended up getting the following:

- A discount on the interest rate
- Several thousand in discounts off the lender broker fees
- $45,000 in additional funding that almost offset the twelve months of interest-only we lost

This new deal ended up being better, and because we underwrote conservatively, we handled it without the concessions. The key point here is that issues will almost always come up, but you should never settle. Always fight for your investors and your deal and negotiate hard.

We literally went down to the wire on this closing, but with a great team and a ton of hours in, we made it happen. After closing, our property management team hit the ground running and quickly started rocking out our business plan. We stayed very close to our new manager, even though we had a district manager above her. We did this to understand her wants and needs so we could help her as much as possible. The also eliminated too much "lost in translation" stuff that always happened when there are too many people involved.

Focus on the Big Picture

There were times when the deal fell out of contract. After all the work we put in, I thought, *Well, that was all for nothing—hundreds of hours just gone.* There were many times when they would just go silent for a week at a time. I would be, like, "Hey, are you going to get back to me? I need an answer to this question." It was very, very challenging. It was great to build up that psychological strength, knowing that this is just the type of process you might go through when you're dealing directly with a private seller.

Emotionally, you have ups and downs. We're human beings, as much as you want to take emotion out of it. It can get difficult. But you really have to focus on the big picture and stay focused on that. You have to work to solve the problems. You have to focus on not being a victim, and just think to yourself, *I'm not going to get caught up in these challenges.* In my own head, I'm going to focus on each particular task—

on how I'm going to solve each problem and how I'm going to execute each task one at a time to close a successful deal. Again, even in your own mind, that's an objective you have to face. That's a challenge. These are obstacles you have to overcome.

Winning the Deal

I think where we really won in this deal was that I got to a point where I said to them, "You're going to have to provide all these things that I'm asking for." This was months and months in, and I said: "The economy is changing. We are facing several challenges with several unknowns. I am willing to come out there and help you do all this stuff. I'm willing to help you build all these documents out, build the pro formas, T-12s, whatever the bank is looking for, and I'm willing to work with you directly to make it as easy as possible."

Once you have a connection with someone, that's where you win. That happened when I could actually deal directly with the seller, because then we could have results-oriented conversations together on the phone. There was a bit of common ground, and once we identified it, we both wanted to get to the finish line without any loss in translation. That is really difficult to do when you're not dealing directly with the seller, because the brokers break that connection—it's just numbers for them, no personal connection there. So it's important to articulate your story and your reasoning once you connect directly, then try to develop a personal connection if at all possible.

They were reluctant every time I would go back and create another storyline based on what we needed or where we were at. When they said, "No, we're not doing it," I said, "Well, then I guess the deal is just going to fall apart." And I stepped back. That's when you have to know when to call a pause. Then after giving them some time, I explained to them what we would need to proceed with the deal and why we needed it. At that point, they realized, "You know what? This guy is going to get us to the finish line." That's how we eventually got there—slow and steady.

Chapter 17
Unforeseen Issues
after Closing

One of the realities of owning class-C workforce housing apartments is that things are bound to (and do) happen that you may not see coming. It's really important to prepare for the unexpected and be able to roll with the punches. This is not to say these properties are the only ones with challenges or challenging tenants—no way, they all have challenges, but you see them more often in this asset class.

Tenant Shooting

In our case, right after closing, we got a call from the police department informing us of a shooting about a week before the sale that the seller did not disclose.

We found out that the shooting was a result of a tenant's son who did not live at the property but tried to rob someone and was instead shot as a result. He was arrested in the hospital because he had a warrant. What? Just what we need, but at least no lives were lost!

This was definitely unfortunate, but it's one of those things you must expect from multifamily apartment complexes in a challenging neighborhood. We had budgeted for things like security, lighting, perimeter fencing, and a camera system, so it was not as concerning as it could have been had we not expected issues.

But that's not all!

Fire Renovations

If you recall the fire that happened earlier on in the deal, the owner had not pulled permits to do the repairs because the city said they were not necessary (we verified that later). But during our questioning, we missed some very crucial details that, had we been specific enough in our questioning, would have saved us time and money.

We were told no permit was required; however, there was a bit of fine print that I hadn't asked about and wasn't disclosed to me: In this county, anytime 911 is called due to a fire, the power company is required to disconnect power to the unit. And before power can be restored, the city must sign off that the unit is in a condition that won't cause the fire issue again once the power is turned back on. The only way to do this is to pull a permit for the specific circumstances and have the city sign off.

Since the city never inquired as to whether the power had been shut off due to a 911 call, it never came up in my questioning about whether permits were required. And it resulted in our simple renovation being turned into a full renovation down to the studs so the city could sign off on the permit. I know this sounds crazy, but these are the little details that can get out of hand, especially when the government and code enforcement get involved. Thankfully, we had enough reserves set aside for unforeseen issues that could arise, but the result was the unit would be out of commission for ten weeks.

The point here is that you must cover every angle you can think of prior to closing, because once you own the property, you are responsible for dealing with every outcome or challenge, no matter how big or small. Do not force a deal and think you can just figure it out afterward. This could have been a big problem, but careful planning and conservative underwriting insulated us.

So for your own reference, if you ever come across a fire or potential code violation during closing, try to speak directly with the code violations and permit engineer to confirm that the work or issues will not require approval or permits to close, and *be specific*. Also, always check with the utility companies as to their experience when dealing with your specific circumstance.

If this cannot happen for some reason, or you are never told of the issues, and it comes up after closing, just be proactive and set aside or raise enough extra funds to cover what you think the worst-case scenario might be in a value-add property. The best problem you could ever have is to have too much capital after closing.

Drugs and Guns

Another issue we found out about while knocking out some of the deferred maintenance repairs in a unit was the presence of drugs and a gun. Once again, we had to contact the authorities, and the tenants were dealt with accordingly, and thankfully, the tenants were already being evicted. But again, be prepared for these types of things to happen. This state had an open-carry law in place, which allows law-abiding citizens to carry a weapon without a permit, so it was not uncommon to see a weapon in the home. But drugs on the properties should not be tolerated. The good news that came out of this is that the word got out to a few other tenants that we would not tolerate this kind of behavior, and they promptly moved on shortly thereafter. This saved us some time and money as it's likely they would have caused issues when evicted.

More Guns

There was a call about two rifles on the outside of an apartment. A neighbor reported that two young people were out in front with weapons. At first, it sounded alarming. These people had weapons, and our policy was no weapons on site, no fighting, and no tolerance for violence at all. So our property management company was going to evict the person who had these people in front of his unit who were associated with him and that he was talking to. But it was during COVID, and we couldn't necessarily evict him, even with this violation of policy.

So for months and months, he stopped paying rent and started talking to other tenants, and they stopped paying rent, and we couldn't evict any of them. But the property management company was steadfast in sticking to their policy and going to court and trying to continue to evict him. So I requested a meeting with him and went to the property and met with him. I wanted to understand his circumstances because before that, we had no issues with him. This was shortly after we took over the property. In talking with him, he said, "Listen, these people came to my property, but they were not affiliated with me. Yes, I happened to talk to them out front. But this is an open-carry state. You can carry a weapon outside in the state of Georgia." So they weren't breaking any laws, and there were no criminal charges after the police came out and spoke with them. I told him, "I'll tell you what. We'll let you stay for six months. And after six months, if there are no issues, then we will re-up your lease at the higher rate. But you need to back-pay all of the rent you owe us." This was approximately four months' rent. We also had cameras at this point that allowed us to see all the activity around his unit.

Well, guess what? Four months later, he had paid all his rent, and the other tenants who were protesting started paying their rent. We never had a problem with him again or any reported incidents like the one that caused all this fuss. So we ended up creating revenue and solving a problem by dealing directly with people and being open-minded versus being judgmental, and sticking to our guns and policies, no pun intended, which we could have done. We were dealing with real people with real challenges, and sometimes that requires clear communication and understanding of one another. The reality is that he and those other tenants could have stayed there paying no rent for probably another nine months because the COVID rules didn't allow for evictions for about nine to twelve months. So how much rent would we have lost if they had decided to just stick it out? We solved the problem by understanding the people and listening to the other side, and it worked out just fine. Sometimes you need to mix up the personalities to overcome conflict.

Enough about all the challenges! Next, we will discuss performance and how to make profits.

Chapter 18
Penny-Wise and Pound-Foolish—Beware of Subcontractors

You are likely better off hiring a general contractor or bringing it all in-house versus hiring subcontractors. Here, I want to give you some examples as to why it's so important to carefully consider hiring a general contractor when starting your value-add property renovations. We experienced the hard way what kind of value a contractor can bring when they are overseeing all the subcontractors and projects that you have during these massive projects.

Shady Subcontractors

I'll list a few examples of subcontractors we dealt with during our various projects with our value-add renovation process. When first touring the property, we came across an individual—we'll call him Mako. He was actually a tenant in the property who was complaining about some deferred maintenance and had offered to either come on board as a full-time maintenance guy for the property or to help with projects. He even offered to renovate the unit he was living in as there was some deferred maintenance that could potentially cause hazards or some form of code violation. Upon further review of his credentials and background, we realized that his work was not going to meet the most basic of standards to accomplish the objectives. It so happened that Mr. Mako was actually four months behind on his rent, a situation I was not aware of when he approached me outside of the property during one of our tours.

Subsequently, he was evicted. And after a few months of back and forth, he moved out when the sheriffs were one day away from physically removing him. Unfortunately, this would not be the last time we crossed paths with Mr. Mako. He came back to that unit and stole tools from the contractors as they were fully renovating units. A few weeks after his departure, we caught Mr. Mako on our camera systems as he came back to the property several times to steal things. Unfortunately, we never physically caught him in the act, and eventually, it stopped. But this was quite a bad experience. What a first impression with one of the tenants on the property!

Check References

So the lesson here is to fully vet anyone who says they're going to do work for you on your property, especially if they're an existing tenant. I would encourage you to never hire somebody and trade rent for work performance within your property. Next, we had a subcontractor we'll call Frank. Frank was working on the property when we took over, so we thought we would give him a shot. Mr. Frank said he could provide endless amounts of labor and good-quality work. But unfortunately, we would find that Mr. Frank didn't have the appropriate licenses to complete the work he said he could complete and really was just more of a glorified handyman. His jobs sometimes would take four to six weeks longer. The excuses would range from him saying the workers didn't show up to him being unable to get supplies. He'd say he was finished even though it wasn't meeting the most basic of standards.

There were instances where he would have to come back three times and fix the problems that he never completed in the first place. This caused major setbacks, time constraints, and additional costs. In some instances, other contractors had to come and finish his work to the quality standard that we expected.

Next, we had a couple of knuckleheads we'll call Mike and Ike. These guys were referred to us by the brother of a guy who was referred to us in the real estate industry. This is a relationship business. And it's always good when you can get referrals from people that you know, especially when labor is a major constraint during a pandemic. Always ask for multiple references and ask those references for a reference that may know your contractor that you were not given by the contractor.

Mike and Ike came to us with an aggressive bid to do some work on a unit renovation, which included things like fixing leaks in the ceiling from previous roof leaks, replacing the cabinets, and painting, just to name a few. But suspiciously, the costs kept climbing after the initial bid. We asked these two approximately how many hours they had worked on the site to reach their final price. When we finally asked them to break down their hourly rates and cost of materials, we were even more suspicious as the hourly rate was twice as much as the market was demanding. We decided to pull up the camera footage and painstakingly review all of it at the time they were on site. It was no surprise that their hours were cut in half.

After negotiating down the hourly rate to market plus a little more, we were paying about 40% less than they initially tried to charge. Again, a lesson to be learned here is, regardless of the referrals, even if they're personal referrals, you still have to do your due diligence. You have to interview references, maybe meet with people in person, and make sure that you have previous work that is proof of what they can do. Show up unannounced, track their work, and more. These guys were a little bit newer in the business and were just throwing numbers out there. They were pulling them out of a hat. They really had no idea how to charge, and their work was lackluster anyway. So we didn't get one pulled over on us on that one. We actually came out okay.

Ultimately, we found a great property maintenance manager who was able to help us manage our subcontractors and get the complex in great shape and keep it there. However, the challenges we faced in getting to that point demonstrated why value-add properties typically require significant hands-on management to reach their full potential. In some cases, a decision can be made to bring renovation and general construction in-house, but you would need enough scale to do this. I would recommend at least 1,500 to 2,000 units under your management umbrella before you consider starting a construction company.

Let's take a moment and talk about communication. This is one of the most important aspects of running any business, but our focus is specifically as it relates to contractors and employees or partners.

Here's what Pumble said in a post regarding stats on workplace communication:

Workplace communication statistics (2022)

Workplace communication statistics show that 86% of employees and executives cite the lack of effective collaboration and communication as the main causes for workplace failures.[22]

On the other hand, teams who communicate effectively may increase their productivity by as much as 25%.

Here are all the interesting facts, figures, and statistics about workplace communication that will help you better grasp why effective workplace communication is important in helping businesses thrive.

Proper communication within a business brings several benefits to the said business.

Studies, reports, and research show effective team communication positively affects employees in terms of the following:

- Productivity
- Engagement
- Retention
- Trust

Effective communication increases productivity.

According to the Connected Culture report, 71% of those employees who said they were more productive feel well-connected to their colleagues. So, employees who regularly communicate with one another are more productive.[23]

Namely, according to a McKinsey report, well-connected teams see a productivity increase of 20–25%.[24]

So good practices in this area involve setting regular meetings with your team, including important contractors and suppliers. Record video meetings when possible. Review all completion dates regularly, and ask if anyone on the team sees potential holdups. Software like ClickUp™ or Monday.com is available to help you manage the process.

Next, I will dive into outperforming your pro forma and how this starts from the beginning or time of acquisition but is a work in progress during the entire time you hold the property.

Chapter 19
How to Outperform
Your Pro Forma

Outperforming your projections starts with conservative underwriting. Here are some key underwriting factors you want to consider.

Rent Escalation

What is your rent escalation plan? Are you bumping rents in an achievable manner, or are you escalating them to meet a specific return you are trying to achieve for you and your investors? Are you relying on a conservative market rent escalation at a 2% to 3% increase each year, or are you being too aggressive so you can compensate for economic conditions, or because you're not hitting the right returns you want in your initial underwriting?

If you want to be conservative, you may want to underwrite with little to no rent escalation, or at the very least, cut it in half from what the offering memorandum states is possible, which is usually higher than 5%.

After you acquire the property, don't be afraid to push rents until your leads start to push back or drop off. You must do this if you do not have market rent adjustment software like RealPage, Yardi Matrix, or others that can guide your decisions. I recommend testing anyway, because a software that is 100% accurate does not exist.

Utilities and Expenses

Have you called the utility companies to confirm the average cost on the building? Did you add extra expenses in your underwriting or at least increase the expenses in the offering memorandum just to be safe? Is there anything you can do to lower these costs? Can you get LED conversions or install energy efficient appliances?

I recommend adding at least 1% to 3% to your overall expenses as a safety buffer.

Are you looking at charging a trash, pest control fee or RUBS (ratio utility billing system, which adds the total cost for utilities and bills each unit a percentage based on square footage, number of residents, number of bedrooms, bathrooms or other factors)?

Replacement Reserves and Maintenance

Do you have enough in replacement and reserves and in your maintenance budget?

I recommend underwriting to $300 per door in heavy value-add or deferred maintenance buildings. It could be as high as $600 per door for replacement reserves per year. This reserve will cover replacement expenses like carpet, HVAC, or roofs.

For maintenance, I recommend at least $50 per door per month, but again, on a heavy-lift or deferred maintenance building, you might go as high as $75 or more.

Underwriting without a Refinance Option

It can be tempting to underwrite your offering with a refinance for several reasons, the two most common ones being:

1. You can increase the IRR (internal rate of return) for investors by maximizing the time value of money and showing a higher IRR with the return of capital.
2. You can push up the cash-on-cash, or perception of the cash-on-cash return, when using some of the underwriting tools I've seen. In other words, it looks better on paper to include a refinance.

There is nothing wrong with refinancing, but remember, most of your investors don't invest to get their money back in two or even three years. They know there will be a gap in time to redeploy that capital, and that's not usually factored in by passive investors when they review the underwriting.

My advice is to underwrite with and without a refinance so you can see the difference. If your deal is still producing solid returns after taking the refinance out, you likely have a solid deal.

Other Income

You may be tempted to build in all the possible options you can to add income to this property and include it in your offering to boost returns, but I would hold some back if you can. This will put you in a stronger position to outperform your pro forma. This also keeps expectations in check.

Examples of other income on a C or B-class property include but are not limited to the following:

- Adding an extra apartment
- Adding an extra bedroom or a den conversion to a bedroom in the apartment
- Dog washing stations
- Adding pet fees
- Community cable or Internet
- Charge a small garbage fee
- Utility bill back or RUBS
- Install water conservation systems (lower expenses)
- Wi-Fi
- Storage

By increasing the income generated by just $10,000 per year, you could increase the value of your property by $175,438 at a 5.7% cap rate.

We encountered many challenges along the way, but one of the most important elements of us not only getting through every day but also outperforming our pro forma was this: We always communicated constantly down to the on-site property management level, even though we had a district manager and higher-level staff we were supposed to go through. We even worked with the maintenance staff on the phone and on-site. We overcommunicated, and this was important because we had real-time information and connection to the asset and all of the nuances that came with it every day.

Now that I've laid out some of the performance variables, let's see how all this worked out at sale. A lot can get lost in translation and personalities can obscure what's really going on. Most people just want to be heard and respected and if you can deliver on that need, then you can run a successful company. We stayed on top of tenant complaints, worked with the city council on a regular basis to solve problems and better the living environment for our tenants. I personally spoke with tenants during my visits, and sometimes they just wanted to be heard. They really appreciated that. We regularly created win-wins with management and tenants that oftentimes were just personality conflicts.

I don't want to sugarcoat this. We had many challenges along the way, like sewer line issues and human waste literally flowing down driveways (tenants had a habit of taking clean out caps off when their grease clogged the lines, and this caused raw sewage to flow down driveways—disgusting!). There's nothing like a property visit on a balmy ninety-eight-degree southern state day with sewage in the air. We had kids vandalizing units, tree limbs falling though roofs twice, and some things too graphic to describe, but we got through all of it together.

Make no mistake, we had a rock star on-site manager. She was confident, tough, and hardworking. Her husband happened to be a contractor as well, which helped bail us out of binds a few times. This was her first property management job, and she crushed it. I'm not sure how we could have done it without her tenacity. Whether it was hawking the cameras, being tough on the troublesome tenants, or her long, dedicated hours and amazing attitude, she was special. She called me well after the sale of the property and said she really appreciated the way we treated her and how on top of things we were. She said we made that experience much easier on her despite the challenging environment. This goes to show that with the right support and constant communication, you can make things happen. My team was literally an extension of her, and we made sure she knew it. Always take care of your frontline people even if they are not hitting their goals with the management company to earn a bonus. Trust me, this makes a big difference.

Chapter 20
The Sale Twelve
Months after
Acquisition

Wow, what a difference a year makes! Can you believe that all that stuff happened in just one year? So here we are, at a crossroads. Ten months in, and we have not only blown through $650,000 worth of CapEx that we budgeted, which included all of the original lender reserve we were given back and then some, but we also unexpectedly exceeded the income level projected in the year one pro forma. We actually hit year three of the pro forma in the first ten months, all while lowering expenses to a rate below the five-year projections. These are crazy numbers, people!

The numbers above would be great on their own, but the last few years have not been what we would call a traditional market for real estate. There were many factors at play in 2020–2021 that made owning a multifamily asset challenging and rewarding beyond what a normal cycle might yield.

Some of the challenges over those months we feel were mostly related to the pandemic, like finding employees and contractors. When you did find someone, it was almost impossible to keep them focused and working. Turnover was insane. As mentioned earlier, we literally paid someone 30% more than market rate for a maintenance position and gave them a sign-on bonus after sixty days, and they did not even make it to thirty-two days.

Some of the benefits of owning at this time were credited to an aggressive purchase price with lower-than-average rents at acquisition, limited inventory, demand for housing, and inflationary factors, causing the value of this asset to go through the roof. This is, in part, based on our income from the property rising well beyond average levels because of things like rent increases.

Exploring Opportunities with the Brokers

We made the decision to discuss selling the property with our brokers, but these brokers were not the original brokers we made this purchase through. This is not normal practice. It's common to reward the brokers you have transacted with on the buy to also award them the sell when ready. But due to the challenges we experienced when we bought, and the experience and effort put forth by the brokers we bought from, after this deal, we felt this was the right decision for our sale. This was a big brokerage with very professional materials to help them sell and a vast network. This decision would pay off big for our investors.

Just sixteen months after acquiring the property, we had to choose whether to hold on to the asset and keep cash flowing, but we would likely need to infuse some cash into it if we wanted to continue to push the rent up. Or we could sell; selling would net significant, higher than projected returns with an early exit for our investors, and the market was still climbing. You cannot time the market, so if you are outperforming your projections, you should consider selling if it benefits your investors.

The decision was made to meet up with the brokers and discuss the options. We sent them the current financials, a rent roll, and T-12. We had a target of around $60,000 to $63,000 at sale per door in year three after our planed CapEx renovation plan was complete, but remember, we finished this in ten months. And of course, we planned for a hold of at least five years, just in case, and on top of that, we secured ten-year stabilized debt so we could hold even longer if needed.

We knew rents were continuing to climb, and as a result, the values of the properties were increasing, but we were surprised at how much when we received our estimated value and sales price per door at exit from the brokers. There was a slight pause by most buyers during the pandemic, but we kept buying and stuck with our plans. The result of sticking with the pre-pandemic plan put us in a position of owning a few great properties nearing completion while many investors started looking for properties to park their money in. We would go on to buy nine properties during the COVID pandemic. The only problem for buyers at this time was that an inventory-constrained market got even tighter and, accompanied by other factors mentioned earlier, created the perfect environment for a value-add seller to maximize profits.

The market we were in with this specific property had at least twenty sales in the past twelve months and none with equal comparisons sold for under $100,000 per door—that's right, $100,000 per door. Our brokers projected that this property would sell in the high $80,000 to low $90,000 per door price range. Using an average of the estimated selling price, that's at least 28% higher than we projected the property to sell at the end of year three of ownership, and this was conservative. We had purchased several properties at the time, and every one of them we bought for above listing price, but of course, they still perform. It was just a sign of the times. For all of you who hate math—that was about a $9.6 million valuation using market cap on a property that was purchased for $3.875 million a year earlier. Market cap is only one factor. Income is among others that are important to consider.

The great thing about this property was that there was still major upside for the purchaser, as there were approximately 70% of the units to renovate and some exterior work, but nothing major to be done. With rents of $900 per month proving the concept and a few tested at $1,000, there was nothing but upside for a potential buyer, even with a $500,000 to $1 million CaPex budget and a three to five--year exit plan.

Let's Do It! Time to Sell!

After careful consideration, we made the call to put the opportunity into the broker's hands and list. He wanted to feel out the level of interest with a select few key buyers before going to the market. The price was approximately $11 million as a pocket listing. This is what you would consider an off-market deal, or a whisper deal, as it had not been officially sent out to the larger market. We also considered this the first attempt at a preemptive deal opportunity for a few to grab it up for a quick close, avoiding the bidding war you see in these hot markets.

For one reason or another, the first two LOIs (letters of intent from interested buyers) that came in around the $11-million mark did not move forward after touring. Now this can be for a number of reasons; some are listed below:

1. A group cannot secure funding in a specific market.
2. There is more CapEx than they anticipated, causing the deal to not pencil in.
3. There was a time-sensitive 1031 exchange (an opportunity to defer capital gains on federal taxes) that will not pencil in with the time constraints.
4. The buyer may feel that the final price will be higher by final LOI acceptance and cannot go any higher than the initial offer.
5. Maybe the property itself or the environment leads a group to pull back after the on-site visit like crime, gas station proximity, or dry cleaners close by.
6. Some inexperienced groups may put an LOI out just to lock up a property, only to realize they cannot raise the funds to close or make the deal work.

There are many reasons, but you want to consider these things when you are buying and when you are selling, as they may limit your ability to achieve a maximum return.

Within a week or so, our brokers extended the whisper list to a larger group, but still not on the open market as the offering memorandum was being prepared.

This group returned with four offers, or LOIs.

Among these offers was a qualified group that came in with an offer of $11.950 million and $300,000 down, with $250,000 of this hard on day one of executing the PSA. When a group puts money down hard, they are serious and have done enough research ahead of time. The money is nonrefundable no matter what after the signing of the PSA, and that signing is usually no later than within two weeks of the acceptance of the LOI.

This offer also included the traditional sixty days to close with a thirty-day extension option by paying an additional $100,000 down nonrefundable.

This offer, once the PSA is signed, is at $105,752 per door. That's approximately 60% higher than the year-five pro forma, which was at $63,000 per door. Remember, we were only about sixteen months in from our original acquisition of the property at this point, and we were sitting with an offer that was 60% higher than the year-five pro forma—that's a really good number. What is interesting is that you could build a pro forma full of projections setting you up for success at sale, and if you reach or exceed them, nice work! But an inspired buyer will use future rents in their buying pro forma if you have proven you can get high rents in a few units. This, if the buyers can get debt, will give them confidence that they can buy at a higher price based on the proof of concept for higher rent.

We have been in the buying position many times and know that things can change after you start the courting process with a broker. The actual offer or LOI you put out will not always be what you eventually pay for the property, even if you are among the limited few in the whisper phase of the purchase, so don't get disappointed if you end up paying more. Just prepare for anything and underwrite to multiple purchase prices ahead of time.

Once you get a good LOI accepted, it's time to engage your counsel so they can prepare the PSA for the buyer. Sometimes, the sellers will want to provide the PSA, and you will have to make the call on it if you will accept that and send it to your attorneys or insist on your own. You will send that over as soon as it's ready, and this is usually about a week after you start the process with counsel.

Use this time you have now to prepare the customary documents you know you will need to provide to the buyer. A good broker team usually will start this for you with a shared Dropbox account getting you ready. But this is important because once the PSA is signed by both parties, there are important deadlines you must adhere to so you're not in breach of contract. Don't assume anyone is going to keep you on track—you and your team must stay organized and on top of all important dates and deadlines. I recommend adding notifications in your phone as meeting invites to each team member noting the topics and time they are due, in addition to software tracking, just to be extra diligent and so you don't miss something.

When selling your property, here is a list of some of the items you may be expected to share with a buyer within five days of the signing of the PSA:

- Copies of financial statements for the property, including up-to-date income and expense statements for two years.
- Copies of service contracts.
- Copies of utility bills.
- An inventory of the personal property.
- Copies of any existing environmental reports if available, geological reports, soils reports, engineering reports, appraisal, probable maximum loss reports, market studies, appraisals, or any

other reports, studies, or surveys pertaining to the property.

- A current commitment for title insurance covering the property issued by the title company and copies of all items referred to in it, along with a copy of the survey of the property.
- A current rent roll for the property indicating, by tenant, the required monthly rental, the deposits, any delinquencies, any prepaid rents and the term. The tenant leases and the tenant files may need to be available at the property or the management company's office for inspection and photocopying.
- Tax statements applicable to the previous tax year.

Exceeding Projections

You may find yourself in a situation where the value to a buyer of what you are selling actually exceeds the price you are selling it for. In other words, a potential buyer sees future value far higher than the price you are asking for it. That actually happened with us on this sale. We thought we were going to get a certain amount, and a new buyer came along and said, "Nope, I'm willing to pay this." And they actually bought it at that price, which was far higher than we thought it would sell for. Now, in most cases, this is because the buyer feels they can build a business plan that will meet or exceed a much higher future value.

I will give you a quick example: Let's say before the sale, you test rents at $1,000 per month, but your going rents are $900. Then you actually get $1,000. If you had a few of these in your rent roll, the buyer may think they can not only reach those rents but also maybe even higher, so they are willing to pay that price. Of course, they still have to convince a lender to give them the money to buy it, and this strategy is not always good enough. They may need to raise more money to pay the higher price, but in their mind, it will be worth it once they get in and execute their plan.

A little color on the original projections when we acquired this property: We originally had projected a hold time of about sixty months, so we were going to hold the property for about five years. We thought, based on the purchase price of $3.875 million, we would actually sell it for around $7.1 million or so in sixty months; we actually ended up selling it for $11.950 million. That ended up being approximately 40% over what we thought we would sell it for in year five, and we did it in just eighteen months, which was amazing. We had an internal rate of return estimate of 14% to 16%; we actually ended up with an IRR at sale of over 85%, which was staggering. We had an average annual cash-on-cash return estimate of 18% to 20%. And we actually at sale delivered a return of over 103% cash-on-cash return.

We had a projection to double the sale price in five years. But in fact, we more than tripled it in eighteen months. So our initial equity multiple was 1.9 to 2.1, and we actually hit an equity multiple of 2.559 in just eighteen months. So this property absolutely way outperformed our initial projections. There were several factors that helped us get there: We executed the plan really quickly. We got creative with additional income (adding a $10 trash fee, enforcing the $10 pet fee, and converting an old owner's suite above the office into a $750/month unit) while lowering expenses. We were assisted by a hot market, which caused several buyers to come in at the last minute and beat each other up. We bought in a very good area for growth. Although it was a challenging market because of crime, once we pushed the criminals out of our building, it not only made a big difference in the tenant experience but also allowed us to over-deliver on our promise to investors.

We went on to buy and sell several value-add deals in the B and C-class space. We learned a lot from each property. We eventually dipped our toe into the development space and found that to be quite scalable and highly profitable for everyone involved, so we made a bit of a pivot, although we still shop value-add.

As we wind down with the basics of how to build a syndication business and the real story of a challenging value-add deal from acquisition to sale, I want to touch on real estate funds and how starting funds helped us scale our capital raises.

Chapter 21
Real Estate Funds

Expanding Our Scope

I want to start this section by sharing a good article by SmartAsset.com of what a real estate fund is.[28]

Real Estate Funds Explained

To understand what a real estate fund is, you first have to know how a mutual fund works. Simply put, a mutual fund is a single collection of several different investments. For example, a fund may own a mix of stocks and bonds, or track the stocks in a particular index, such as the S&P 500 or the Dow Jones Industrial Average.

A real estate fund works similarly, except it only invests in real estate (either directly or indirectly). A real estate fund may own individual commercial properties, for instance, or invest in a collection of properties (think shopping centers and hotels). A real estate fund can also invest in Real Estate Investment Trusts, or REITs.

Real estate funds can be open-end or closed-end. An open-end fund allows you to enter or leave the fund as long as it remains active. A closed-end fund typically has one entry point and one exit point; you have to invest within a certain window and, once invested, cannot leave the fund until it's run through its natural life cycle.

Like any other mutual fund, real estate funds can be passive or actively managed. Passive investment strategies typically try to mimic the performance of an underlying index. Take, for example, the Vanguard Real Estate Index Fund. The VGSIX, as it's known, tracks the performance of the MSCI US REIT Index, which in its own right tracks domestic equity REITs.

With an actively managed investment strategy, the fund manager oversees the buying and selling of the underlying assets within the fund. Instead of trying to match the performance of an underlying index, actively managed funds attempt to beat it. The Cohen & Steers Global Realty Shares Fund (CSFAX) is one example of a real estate fund that relies on an active management strategy to drive investor returns.

So What's the Difference between a Real Estate Fund and a REIT?

One primary difference between a REIT and a real estate fund is that a REIT is a corporation, which is traded like a stock. REITs are required to pay out 90% of their taxable income to investors. So a REIT is attractive to investors looking to generate income. Other benefits of property ownership, such as depreciation, can also be realized by investing in a REIT. Many REITs have very specific targets for what they invest in, such as office space in large cities, while others take a broader approach, like any leased space in different industries and geographies.

A real estate fund, on the other hand, collects money from a group of investors, usually through an online brokerage, and investors pay a flat expense fee every year. Some real estate funds also pay out periodic dividends to investors, although there is no legal requirement to do it.

The fund structure we chose to go with is a real estate fund. This is basically a pool of money that we invest in the projects we develop with our partners. Limited partner investors share in the profits because our fund is a partner in the development projects. This is not a REIT as described above.

We started our new construction fund in 2022 and will start breaking ground in 2023 on our projects. We started building out the fund structure in 2022. It takes time, anywhere from, let's say, three to six months to build out your fund, unless you're using a crowdfunding platform; in that case, you're looking at maybe four to eight weeks. If you are looking to start a fund, you should understand it's not only going to cost money, specifically attorney cost, but it will also take time. Starting a fund could cost as little as $6,500 up to $100,000 or more. Then when that's done, you're ready to start raising money. You could also start a CF or crowdfunding fund on its own to have access to unlimited nonaccredited investors that you can advertise to, and that gives you lots of flexibility. See Silicon Prairie for more on CF funds.

When we raise for a new construction project, we start raising money well before the construction starts, so you might want to start raising money for your new project anywhere from six to nine months before you start.

For our new development projects, we partnered with the developer we worked with before on a previous project. We did that before we even began raising capital. That project we had a previous partnership on was just finishing completion; it started two and a half years before. So we knew a sound model and proof of concept was there.

We decided to expand our scope in new development for two reasons: First, because we knew this quality of product would draw in great lender rates and private equity and, in some cases, be easier to sell as larger firms seek them out. This, in turn, would allow us to deliver stabilized returns for our investors while partnering on luxury apartments with the latest amenities. And two, with rising interest rates and sellers still trying to get a premium for their properties, it was becoming more difficult to provide the type of returns that our investors expected. That's not to say opportunities are not out there in the value-add space. I have friends buying value-add now, and they are finding some good deals, but they are far and few between. There are always opportunities everywhere in every market, but it takes a lot of work to find them today. I'm also seeing sponsors of deals shifting to starting debt funds with raised capital versus buying properties like they were. In other words, they are raising money to then lend on behalf of their investors.

One last thing on funds: A fund allows you to raise money continuously. So instead of having to raise in a very tight timeline on a value-add deal or direct syndication, you generally have 60, 90 or maybe 120 days at max to raise all your money; you can raise money in a fund whether it's 30 days or even up to a year or longer. There are different structures of funds that take the pressure off raising all that money in a really short period of time, especially in new construction multi-property project, because you would be starting the construction at different time frames per property. One construction project may start in six months, the next one starts in ten months, and the next one starts in twelve months, which is why you have a longer investment time frame as well. So it just gives you a little more flexibility if you have a fund with an extended capital raising period.

Takeaways

I know I covered a lot in this book, but I would like to leave you with a few things to consider when you take over a challenged property or jump into the development space:

- Seek out and partner with people that share your values and work ethic.
- Raise more money than you need, and do not underestimate how hard raising capital can be.
- Always plan for the worst-case scenario.
- There is no substitute for a talented team and asset manager, but a spectacular property management company and manager is about as good as it gets. Choose wisely.
- Don't stress out about situations that are out of your control. Plan for them, and work through the issues with all parties involved.
- Don't just partner with your team and extended team. Partner with local law enforcement, city council, and community leaders, if possible, as they may become great allies.
- Remember you are running a business with many moving parts, so don't forget to utilize all the players in your group to execute the best way forward on every task at hand.
- Communicate constantly with your team, contractors, and investors. You can't communicate enough.

- Don't forget about your vendors and contractors. They are worth their weight in gold, and if you have a heavy value-add property, they will make or break you.
- Explore diversifying into different classes of real estate. It's okay to be curious and shift.
- Learn and much as you can about debt and funds.

This property in our value-add story is in much better shape than it was at acquisition. All of the tenants who caused trouble are gone, many of the deferred maintenance issues have been addressed, the property is looking much better, and tenants left great reviews online, indicating they are thankful for the change. The property also outperformed the pro forma and business plan. So despite the chaos and challenges we faced, it worked out for everyone in the end. This could not have been achieved without good partners like Paul Wilcox the co-founder and COO of Sterling Rhino Capital, who stepped up big-time and worked countless hours to keep things moving. I mention how important it was early on to have a good team, and his attitude and work ethic is a prime example of that. This deal would have been hell without him. Thank you, Paul.

Final Thoughts

Deals are like water, always flowing and shifting. You must get creative, explore every viable option, and have two to three different plans of execution for how you will approach the opportunity, so you are ready for anything and can close the deal regardless of the unforeseen circumstances you may face.

Making deals and buying multifamily apartment complexes is not about egos or winning. It's about problem-solving, understanding people, and making profits for your investors. Without calculated compromise and creativity, you can lose a golden opportunity right in front of you, but you must check your ego at the door and work really hard, constantly looking from both a seller's and buyer's perspective.

Be firm but be reasonable. Search for the not-so-obvious solutions, and find a way to the finish line. You may have to find something no one (including your brokers) can see or get very creative in your explanation to sell your position.

Apply these principles, and you will rock your deals!

Go get 'em

If you want to learn more about investing in multifamily apartment complexes, you can join the Sterling Rhino Capital Investor Club here or check out our website at sterlingrhino-capital.com.

Closing Words

Now that we've reached the end of the book, I'd just like to say that I hope you've found the content interesting or at least educational. I've learned a lot about how to make money in real estate over the course of my journey from being a traditional stock market investor to becoming a real estate owner/operator, and I've done my best to share much of what I've learned along the way in this book. The experience has been both rewarding from a financial standpoint and valuable from a personal development perspective. I found that I had it in me to create another source of income that was like what you might make from working a second job. As covered in this book, it actually became my primary source of income once I realized how profitable investing in it could be.

Whether or not you decide to get involved in real estate investing yourself, I sincerely hope you will benefit from reading this book. I believe expanding one's knowledge about different ways to invest and generate wealth is always a worthwhile activity, and I hope you've found that reading this book has been just that.

Notes and References

1. "24 Investing Statistics You Must Know," Financially Simple, Wealthsource, January 2017, https://financiallysimple.com/24-interesting-investing-statistics-you-must-know/

2. "Who Is Winning the Investing Battle of the Sexes, Men or Women?" Financially Simple, Wealthsource, December 2016, https://financiallysimple.com/who-is-winning-the-investing-battle-of-the-sexes-men-or-women/

3. Reid, Jim, et al. "Long-Term Asset Return Study: The Next Financial Crisis," Deutsche Bank Markets Research, September 2017, https://www.tramuntalegria.com/wp-content/uploads/2017/09/Long-Term-Asset-Return-Study-The-Next-Financial-Crisis-db.pdf

4. Rynecki, David. "10 Stocks To Last The Decade," https://money.cnn.com/magazines/fortune/fortune_archive/2000/08/14/285599/index.htm

5. Aragão, Carolina. "Gender pay gap in U.S. hasn't changed much in two decades," March 2023, https://www.pewresearch.org/short-reads/2023/03/01/gender-pay-gap-facts/

6. Your J.P. Morgan Wealth Partner , J.P. Morgan Wealth Management, https://www.jpmorgan.com/wealth-management/wealth-partners

7. "Mortgage Debt: Pay it Off or Invest? Which Should I Do?" Financially Simple, Wealthsource, October2017, https://financiallysimple.com/pay-mortgage-debt-invest/

8. Bieber , Christy. "Workers Are Dangerously Underestimating How Much Income They Need to Replace in Retirement," The Motley Fool, July 2020, https://www.fool.com/retirement/2020/07/28/workers-underestimating-income-need-retirement.aspx.

9. Bieber, Christy. "How Your Spending Is Likely to Change as a Retiree," The Motley Fool, June 2020, https://www.fool.com/retirement/2020/06/05/how-your-spending-likely-change-as-retiree.aspx

10. "The New Social Contract: Age-Friendly Employers," Aegon Retirement Readiness Survey 2020, Aegon N.V. 2020, https://transamericacenter.org/docs/default-source/global-survey-2020/tcrs2020_SR_new-social-contract-age-friendly-employers.pdf

11. Lake, Rebecca. "How to Invest in Multifamily Housing," U.S. News & World Report, August 2019, https://money.usnews.com/investing/real-estate-investments/articles/how-to-invest-in-multifamily-housing.

12. Duggan, Wayne. "5 Tips To Handle Stocks Market Volatility," U.S. News & World Report, December 2018, https://money.usnews.com/investing/stock-market-news/articles/tips-to-handle-stock-market-volatility

13. Lake, Rebecca. "8 Best Apartment REITs to Buy Now," U.S. News & World Report, August 2019, https://money.usnews.com/investing/real-estate-investments/slideshows/best-apartment-reits-to-buy-now

14. Duchene, Patricia. "The Five Values That Great Mentors Share," Forbes, May 2019, https://www.forbes.com/sites/patriciaduchene/2019/05/21/the-five-values-that-great-mentors-share/?sh=1e4c778b5790\

15. Esajian, Paul. "Techniques & Strategies For Raising Real Estate Capital," FortuneBuilders, November 2022, https://www.fortunebuilders.com/how-to-raise-capital-for-real-estate-ventures/.

16. "How to Negotiate: 5 Tips for Negotiating Better," MasterClass, June 2021, https://www.masterclass.com/articles/tips-for-negotiating-better

17. "How to Negotiate: The 5 Stages of the Negotiation Process – 2023," MasterClass, June 2021, https://www.masterclass.com/articles/how-to-negotiate

18. Klaff, Oren. *Pitch Anything*, New York City, NY: McGraw Hill, 2011.

19. Voss, Chris. *Never Split the Difference: Negotiating As If Your Life Depended On It*, New York City, NY: Harper Business, 2016

20. Dawson, Roger. *The Secrets of Power Negotiating*, Newburyport, MA: Career Press, 2021

21. Zaremba, Yauhen. "Why contracts are important and what is their purpose?" PandaDoc Blog, December 2022, https://www.pandadoc.com/blog/why-contracts-are-important/.

22. "Workplace communication statistics (2022)" Pumble.com (2022), https://pumble.com/learn/communication/communication-statistics/.

23. "New Study Reveals Boost in Employee Productivity and Well-Being Among Companies That Foster a 'Connected Culture' in Work from Anywhere Environment," RingCentral, BusinessWire, November2020, https://www.businesswire.com/news/home/20201111005284/en/New-Study-Reveals-Boost-in-Employee-Productivity-and-Well-Being-Among-Companies-That-Foster-a-%E2%80%98Connected-Culture%E2%80%99-in-Work-from-Anywhere-Environment

24. Chui, Michael, et al. "The social economy: Unlocking value and productivity through social technologies," McKinsey Global Institute, July 2012, https://www.mckinsey.com/industries/technology-media-and-telecommunications/our-insights/the-social-economy

25. Alexander, Andrea, et al. "What employees are saying about the future of remote work," McKinsey & Company, April 2021, https://www.mckinsey.com/capabilities/people-and-organizational-performance/our-insights/what-employees-are-saying-about-the-future-of-remote-work

26. Alcala, Lori. "4 Trends in Workplace Communication," CMSWire, January 2015), https://www.cmswire.com/cms/social-business/4-trends-in-workplace-communication-infographic-027762.php

27. Erkic, Ana. "How to break down team silos and improve collaboration," Pumble Blog, July 2022, https://pumble.com/blog/break-down-team-silos/

28. Lake, Rebecca. "What Is a Real Estate Fund?" Smartasset.com, January 2023, https://smartasset.com/investing/real-estate-fund

www.ingramcontent.com/pod-product-compliance
Lightning Source LLC
Chambersburg PA
CBHW071417210326
41597CB00020B/3547